COMMENTS ON *THE PROACTIVE PATH:*

"Outstanding work. Your dynamic positive energy jumps off each page!"
>—Wes Elmer, President, Coca-Cola of Northern New England

"Richard, congratulations. Your book will serve as a guide for people to enhance their personal success."
>—John L. MacKinnon, CEO, Performance Training Associates, Inc.

"The Proactive Path *allows one to become aware, alive, awake to what one may become."*
>—Steve Conroy, President, Boston Electronic Document Co.

"Richard Tosti's book provides a success formula for permanent behavior change in life and work. Your success in life and work accelerates to new heights!"
>—Ken Cieplik, Vice President of Field Sales, Reebok International

"If one needed proof positive for the oft-quoted adage 'If you can conceive it, you can do it,' The Proactive Path *is a must read."*
>—John Geheran, Vice President, Sales Strategy, BOSE Corporation

"The Proactive Path *by Richard Tosti guides me every day. It keeps me focused and reminds me of the enormous returns I can get out of life by doing the simple things right."*
>—Bill Galatis, Executive Vice President, New England Sports Museum, Fleet Center

"Richard, Thank you for sharing your story in The "Proactive Path. *What a motivating and uplifting life you have lived! One can learn so much from your experiences and example."*
>—Albert J. Martella, Vice President, Program Manager, Producer Training, Merrill Lynch

"An outstanding and practical guide to personal development. Richard provides individuals with a guide that combines dynamic motivational tools and in-depth discussions of how to succeed in all aspects of one's personal and professional life into a clear and concise plan of action."
—Tony Venuti, Vice President, CDM

"If you dare to allow yourself to commit to the actions prescribed in this book you will experience both a personal and professional transformation which will lead you to outstanding achievement."
—John C. Hennessy, Senior Vice President, TECH/AID, DMS, Area 1

"The lessons here are persuasive, effective and hard-hitting. I found the book to be inspiring, insightful and a powerful weapon in the arsenal of the modern manager."
—Gerald G. Colella CPM, CPIM, CIRM, Vice President, Global Business Operations, MKS Instruments, Inc.

"I live by CPI3030 that is described in The Proactive Path. *Also, I have attended Richard Tosti's seminars several times and have been listening to Richard's tapes/CD for several years. He can positively influence* your *life. Thanks for influencing mine!"*
—Frank Pierce, Vice President, Customer Services, IKON Office Solutions

"Great insight into People, Performance and Success. Some books are only a reference resource in a bookcase, but this book makes you take action. Richard challenges you to look at your positive and negative abilities and act. The challenge is to have the will and desire to change. Only then can you achieve a level of excellence in your life."
—Dan Donaldson, Vice President, Marketing, Hallsmith-Sysco

"Richard Tosti provides simple but hard hitting advice on how to use success techniques to achieve excellence—to be all you can be, as a leader or in any pursuit to which the reader is truly committed. This guide to achieving personal excellence is easy to read and truly enjoyable."
—William Hunt, Director, Organizational Effectiveness, Raytheon Co.

"Mr. Tosti has gathered the universal truths of personal/professional achievement and presents them with passion and precision in such a way that you are immediately energized. This book is a must for any selling organization that is serious about growth."
>—James F. Bochiechio, Director of Sales, Yellow Book USA.

"Richard Tosti is on the cutting edge of teaching people how to make the transition from being average to becoming an over-achiever. The grace of God, support of my wife, and practical application of Richard's techniques for over 25 years have helped me rise from an unmotivated, college drop-out to a top sales executive position in a $600M company with the privilege of leading 500. The same can happen to anyone else willing to take the journey by following the formula in **The Proactive Path.***"*
>—Timothy A. Fraumann, National Sales Director, UniFirst Corp.

*"***The Proactive Path** *is an excellent compilation on improving your personal/professional performance and acquiring a more optimistic outlook on life. It draws from many experts in the field and adds Richard's unique flair. An easy read that can make a difference!"*
>—Tom McChesney, Director, Sprint Business Enterprise Strategy, Center of Excellence

"What a wonderfully written book. The keys to success at any level are contained within **The Proactive Path.** *Follow the steps to unlock your full potential and the doors will open. Thanks for showing me the way!"*
>—John J. Romano, Industrial Plastics Division Manager, USCO/F.W. Webb Co.

"What I have learned from your teachings is that more important than the goal is the person I have become—a person who can change and save lives through the mission of the Boys and Girls Club. Thank you for showing me the way."
>—Daniel Grabowski, Founder of Boys and Girls Clubs, Blackstone, Milford, Woonsocket

THE PROACTIVE PATH

A Radical Guide
to Business Excellence

A Focus Book by

Richard Josti

Monterey Pacific Publishing
Bandon, Oregon

ISBN 1-880710-98-6

Library of Congress Control Number 2002111152

Cover design by Irene Taylor, it grafx
Typesetting by Barbara Kruger

**Monterey Pacific Publishing
Bandon, Oregon**

I would like to dedicate this book to the graduates of my programs who have walked the talk and continue to live a life of excellence, and who are the role models that inspire me daily. Some are retired and I honor them as well.

Paul Colangelo, Vice President of Human Resources, Muro Pharmaceutical

Bill Hunt, Director of Human Resources, Raytheon Company

John C. Hennessy, Senior Vice President, TAC Worldwide Companies

Jim Fabiano, Executive Manager, TAC Worldwide Companies

Ken Cieplik, Vice President of Sales/Operations, Reebok

Wes C. Elmer, President, Coca-Cola Bottling Company of Northern New England

Ann Marie Lacharite, Director of Human Resources, Coca-Cola of Northern New England

Linda Bailey, Training & Marketing Manager, Bickford's Family Restaurants

Dale Bartels, Director, CSO Americas-3COM

Hank Montinari, Director, Worldwide Escalations, CSO-3COM

Kenneth W. Kerber, Human and Organizational Development, 3COM

John J. Romano, General Manager, USCO/FW Webb Company

Frank Netherwood, Sales Manager, IDG World Expo

Chuck Drogosch, General Manager, Coca-Cola Bottling Company of Michigan

Peter Napoli, Senior Vice President, Colley/McCoy (McDonald's)

Bob C. McDougall, Vice President, Colley/McCoy (McDonald's)

Gary Saucier, Supervisor, Colley/McCoy (McDonald's)

Tony LaGreca, President, Oreck Commercial Sales

Tim A. Fraumann, National Sales Director, Unifirst Corporation

Frank Pierce, Northeast District Vice President Customer Service, IKON

David Leger, Agent, Northwestern Mutual Financial Network

Connell J. Tarr, CLU, ChFC, General Agent, Cornerstone
Financial Group

Craig J. Tomasini, Director of Operations, Fulenwider
Enterprises, Inc.

Sandy Fisher, General Manager, Ricoh/Savin Company

Ron Corsentino, Director, Dealer Division, Savin Corp.
Gestetner Division

Ray Sousa, General Manager, Inskip

Michael J. Bonsignore, Vice President Operations, Consolidated
Container Company

Gary Moulton, Owner/Operator, McDonald's

Cal Fox, Owner Operator, McDonald;s

Doug Quagliaroli, Owner Operator, McDonald's

Jocelyn M. Talbot, Senior Vice President, MONSTER.COM

Martin M. Cohne, CLU, ChFC, Prudential

Mike Brunner, Senior Vice President, Federal Systems Division
AT&T

John M. Little, Manager, Northeast Region Honeywell

Bob Parent, Vice President, Honeywell

John, Herb & Jay Cogliano, Owners, A Sullivan & Cogliano
Company

Willis L. Saulnier, Retired Manager, Training/Development,
Raytheon

Bob Warn, Vice President, Norand Corporation

Dick Eagan, Director, Century 21

Dennis Reed, Director, Regional Director, Century 21

Nelson Zide, Owner, ERA John Nelson Realty, Inc.

Fran G. Daub, Manager, DeWolfe Real Estate,

Tom Harrington, Division Vice President, GM Coca-Cola
Enterprises, Inc. (Lakeshore Division),

Scott Figura, Director of Remanufacturing, Coca-Cola
Enterprises, Inc.

Claire Sheff, Assistant Superintendent, Norwell Public Schools

George Hill, Executive Secretary-Treasurer, Retired, Mass.
Association of School Superintendents

Gabe Simon, Leader of Boys Clubs of America

Carl Brand, President, Northeast Electric Distributors

Mark F. Peterson, President of Eagle Electric Supply Company
Tom Maguire, Vice President, Nextira,
Bob C. Babbitt, Vice President/Sales Operations, Getronics
Rich Litt, Division Vice President, Automatic Data Processing
Joe Andrews,Vice President, HR Progress Software
William P. Galatis, Executive Director, Sports Museum of New
   England
Paul LeBlanc, Vice President of Business Development, Coca-
   Cola of New England
Gary Dumas, Sales Center Manager, Coca-Cola of New England
Dan Brown, President, IKON Northern New England
Bob Hallissy, President, IKON South Florida Market Place
Jim Bochiechio, Director of Training, Yellowbook USA
Art Rico, Field Service Manager, McDonald's Corp.
Daniel Grabowski, President, Blackstone Valley Boys and Girls
   Club
Chuck Parr, Regional Director, Ricoh Corporation
John Wholley, Owner, Better Bedding
Tom Wholley, Owner, Better Bedding
Tom Scott, General Manager, Honda North
Patrick Mahr, Sales Trainer, Solidworks
Jay Novack, Director of Sales, IDG World Expo
Rob Scheschareg, Vice President Sales, IDG World Expo
Kevin Begin, Vice President, Retail Sales, Garelick Farms
Gerald Finn, Vice President of Food Service Sales, Garelick
   Farms
Ed Laders, General Agent, The Principal Finance Group
Paul Bugli, Sales Manager, Paychex
Mary Carfagna, Trainer, United States Postal Service
Fred Muzi, President, Muzi Ford City
Dale Sinesi, Vice President Administration, Muzi Motors
Glenn Cammarano, Chief Operating Officer, Muzi Motors
Bob McCarthy, Account Executive, Advantage Sales &
   Marketing/ESM
David Barton, Vice President, CNT
Dennis Wilcox, Sales Manager, CNT

James B. Connors, Training and Development Manager, United Parcel Service

John Lanotte, Customer Experience Manager, Field Sales, Bose Corporation

Jerry Graves, Former Vice President, CCE

Marcello Celentano, former Area Manager, Enterprise Rent-a-Car

Robert O'Brien, former group manager, Polaroid Express

Charles G. Mascott, CLU-former General Agent, Commonwealth Financial group

Barry David, former President, Northeast Division ADP

Palmer Swanson, former Director of Customer Service, Polaroid

Ted Highberger, former President, Coca-Cola of New England & Coca-Cola of New York

Roger Goodson, Managing Director, Prudential Financial

Michael J. Cole, Senior Training Specialist, U.S. Postal Service

Tom McChesney, Director Sprint Business, Enterprise Strategy

Tony Venuti, Vice President, CDM

John MacKinnon, CEO, Performance Training Associates, Inc.

Al Martella, Vice President, Producer Training, Merrill Lynch

Daniel Grabowski, Founder of Boys & Girls Clubs, Blackstone, Milford, Woonsocket

Steve Conroy, President, Boston Electronic Documents Co.

Gene Charette, CEO, Creative Marketing Concepts, Inc.

Acknowledgments

To the teachers who have made a profound difference in my life. These are my mentors.

Umberto Tosti—Dad, Olga Tosti-Mom, Ralph Waldo Emerson, Napoleon Hill, Dr. Denis Waitley, Stephen Covey, Zig Ziglar, Og Mandino, Maureen Vajdic, David Schwartz, Ph.D., Dale Carnegie, Rudyard Kipling, General Patton, Mike Frank, Brian Tracy, Tony Allessandra, Ph.D., Price Pritchett, Alan Weiss, Phil Max Kay, Dr. Herbert Benson, Earl Nightingale, Nido Qubein, President George W. Bush, Robert H. Schuller, Maxwell Maltz, Tony Robbins, James Allen, Bob Proctor, Jack Welch, Kahlil Gibran, Rick Pitino, Donald Trump, Lou Holtz, Wess Roberts, Kenneth Blanchard, Ph.D., Spencer Johnson, M.D., Jack Canfield, Mark Victor Hansen, Bill Gates, Wayne W. Dyer, Teddy Roosevelt, Michelangelo, Ron Kimball, Dick Grondin.

Contents

x

INTRODUCTION

This book is a compilation of the ideas and the spirit developed and refined from twenty-five years of presentations to major corporations. Far from being traditional or stuffy, these seminars are heart-pounding, spine-tingling and powerfully inspiring presentations to Fortune 500 companies. They are dynamic, outside-the-box, multimedia events with extensive audience participation. The response to them is extraordinary; the ideas, the style of presentation and the powerful motivation techniques cause spontaneous, standing ovations and a determination to succeed that is real and ongoing.

All the important points from these seminars are included in this book, which introduces an entirely new paradigm of thinking and acting. Make no mistake about it. This is not just another self-help book, it is a radical and rapid means of placing yourself on a direct path toward success, and avoiding extinction.

Every business, in every area of industry and commerce, is having to become leaner, more efficient and more generally savvy. If you are not prepared to excel in the coming business environment, prepare for extinction, for there will be less and less room for mediocrity.

This book is for those who opt for excellence, for potential high-achievers only, and for current high-achievers whose visions extend even farther. If you are indifferent to great success, stop here, this isn't for you. But if you are serious—really serious—about beginning to live your grandest dreams and achieving your highest aspirations, and if you are willing to look at a totally unique approach to accomplishing this, please read on.

Stop and think about this for a moment. What causes an athlete to become a champion? What causes a teacher to become an inspiration? What causes a politician to become a great statesman? What causes a soldier to become an outstanding military leader? What causes a businessman or businesswoman to become a dynamic CEO? What do all these high-achievers have in common? Is it family environment? The availability of a proficient mentor? Is it physical skill on the athletic field or organizational skill at soldiering or knowledge of teaching or business acumen? Certainly all of these play a role. But there is something more important that all high-achievers have in common—they are all *Focus 1* and *Focus 2* thinkers, and they all have ample *EQ,* all of which I will explain.

It has been shown that 85% of success in achieving business and personal goals is due to personal characteristics—attitude and thought patterns—while only 15% is due to aptitude, natural talent and technical expertise. Please note this carefully. *High achievers become high achievers not because of how smart they are or how many facts they have learned or what physical skills they have honed, they become high achievers because of how they use their minds!* And they use their minds differently from most of us. *Whether or not you become a high achiever will depend on how you use your mind!*

Assume for a moment that you are highly motivated to succeed—at least you *believe* you are highly motivated. But are you really?

Perhaps you have heard how a baby elephant is circus-trained. It is fastened by the leg to a strong, steel chain. Hundreds of times it moves to the limit of the chain and is then restrained. Five years or so later the elephant weighs two tons. Around its leg is a piece of rope, tied to a wooden stake pegged about two feet into the ground. It could easily break the rope or loosen the stake but it doesn't try to escape *because it doesn't believe it can.* It has been conditioned. It now has self-imposed limitations that govern its behavior.

Like the rest of us, you have probably been conditioned daily by the failures and setbacks, as well as the successes, you've encountered since childhood. Because of negative experiences, a part of you keeps insisting that you are limited in what you can accomplish, and this voice of limitation affects everything you do—whether you like it or not!

Without some new kind of intervention, your mental state in the present is decided by your past, and images in your mind of past achievement, or lack of it, will largely determine your behavior in the present, regardless of how badly you want to succeed.

So before you can actually become a high-achiever, a necessary first step is re-programming yourself, and the secret to doing this effectively is to learn how to change certain ways that you think, feel, see, talk and act.

Now you may already be a natural high-achiever; that is, you may already be constantly re-programming yourself without being aware of it. But if you're like most of us, learning to be mentally proactive is a distinct change from our former behavior in which thoughts, feelings and pictures just float into and out of our minds without our having any control over them. This book describes a powerful system wherein you will be undertaking something new and different; for a part of each day you will be doing *directed* thinking, feeling, seeing, speaking and acting. The effects of this are very far-reaching. Among other benefits, a positive feedback loop is created wherein body chemistry actually changes, and these physical changes support and enhance the new mental procedures undertaken.

I use the term *Focus 1* to describe how future achievements can be imagined/visualized as if they have already occurred. I use *Focus 2* to describe how the rewards of future achievements can be imagined/visualized as if they are even now being enjoyed. One of the purposes of this book is to teach you to use and perfect Focus 1 and Focus 2 thinking. Another facet of this book is about IQ and *EQ*. We're all familiar with the term, Intelligence

Quotient, which in general is our ability to analyze, detect patterns, synthesize and articulate. In recent years psychologists have focused increasingly on what they call EQ, emotional intelligence quotient, which is the capacity to understand and control our own emotions, to correctly identify those of others, and to guide our relationships based on this knowledge. In studies done of achievement and leadership, researchers have found that the higher the position, the more EQ is the determining factor of success. It is not that EQ takes the place of analytical intelligence; it is that analytical intelligence is present in most people but there is an insufficiency of EQ—and both are necessary. So a part of this book addresses the need for EQ and offers a comprehensive approach to enhancing it.

But for all the powerful techniques presented in *The Proactive Path,* no system will work without commitment, and if I am to influence others to make a commitment, I have to understand what leads them to do it and sustain it, and what transpires to break it.

There are many reasons why we don't follow through with good ideas or pursue gainful avenues. Sometimes they are too uncomfortable, too complicated, too inconvenient or too unrealistic. And sometimes, in spite of our best intentions, we simply forget to do them—out of sight, out of mind.

We all have do-it switches in our brains. One of these switches I call a tickle switch. This switch temporarily tickles our motivation, excitement, inspiration or intellectual reasoning; and then most of us revert to our former behavior. But there is another switch that is less accessible, the commitment switch. This switch becomes accessible when we come to a point where we say to ourselves, "Enough!" or "Yes!" or "No!" and we say it in such a way that it is irrevocable. The nature of this switch is that once turned on, it cannot be turned off.

In my seminars that describe these high-achievement performance rituals, the participants get so excited, so inspired and so determined that by the end of the seminar their commitment switches have been turned ON and there is no turning back. I can't replicate the atmosphere of my seminars in this book, but what I have done is to create a support system that delves deeply into the nature of habits and provides an effective methodology for ending bad habits, and gaining and retaining the many new ones described in this book. This support system reminds you, encourages you, inspires you and makes you *want* to do what you know you *should* do, and it is now in the form of this easy to read, easy to do, and most importantly, this *easy to keep on doing* book. In fact, I believe you will find this book so packed with new and exciting content that you, too, will find your commitment switch turned ON.

In addition to the comprehensive, proactive procedures presented and the methodology for changing habits, additional supporting elements are described, such as how to use your newfound skills to create high-achieving, win-win relationships; understanding how certain speech patterns are beneficial and others harmful; how to develop associations with winners; and a host of other support skills.

Although *The Proactive Path* is chock full of new ideas, it is also a practical, hands-on guide to daily activities. The chapters end with Action Steps that enable you to immediately begin using what you have just learned. Most of this book is written in the first person, present tense. There are two reasons for this. One is that I've written this book for myself as well as for you; I use it as my own daily guide and reminder. The other reason is that research has shown that proactive thinking and speaking are most powerful when done in the first person, present tense, and I would like you to become accustomed to doing it in this form.

Is it realistic to state that you can achieve great success by following this program, or is it pie-in-the-sky? Thousands of my successful students are living proof that it really does work. I, myself, was a slow learner and I had to work twice as hard as everyone else in order to succeed.

As a result of following this program, I am now a successful consultant—which reminds me of a story. As a child, my dad once said to me, "Richard, you should eat calves' brains, you'll get smarter." I was in a health food store the other day. Calves' brains were $2 an ounce, accountants' brains were $50 an ounce, lawyers' brains were $100 an ounce and consultants' brains were $1,000,000 an ounce. I asked, "Why is there such a large disparity between accountants', lawyers' and consultants' brains?" The store owner said, "Do you know how many consultants we have to shoot to get an ounce of brains?"

I hope you will read this book with a sense of fun and enthusiasm. I firmly believe it is the most comprehensive, most effective system of self-development ever offered. One of the great pleasures in my life is to watch my students become high-achievers, and I hope you will join them.

How serious are you about succeeding? The tools are right here and right now, within these pages. Opportunity is knocking on your door. Can you hear it? Is anyone home?

Before I close this Introduction, I'd like to say a word about beginners. Like most others, you will be a beginner at the processes described in this book. Beginners can sometimes become impatient with new exercises and procedures. I'd like to relate a brief story told by an associate about being a beginner.

In a group exercise for marketing and sales staff, each of us was given three juggling balls and, after some cursory instructions, we were told to begin juggling. We all wondered what this had to do with business but initially we went along with it. Some of us were more adept than others; I seemed even less skilled than most. After fifteen minutes of constantly dropping balls, I became disgusted and stopped.

The group leader noticed my exasperation, and he came over and asked me how I was doing. I vented my frustration and told him I didn't see the point of it and that I thought it was a waste of time. He then asked me if I thought of myself as a master juggler. I answered, of course not. Then he asked if I was at least a minimally competent juggler, and I again replied in the negative. Then he said that in view of this, shouldn't I expect to be dropping the balls? And he suggested that perhaps a part of my frustration was that I assumed I could learn this skill immediately.

The lesson, of course, was that I was not allowing myself to be a beginner, and that if I did so I would not only be less frustrated but would learn more quickly. Now, whenever I am challenged with a new business problem I remember my first attempt at juggling, and realize I am a beginner.

As you begin this new and exciting process of learning to proactively direct yourself toward high achievement, I ask you to do the same.

1

My Judge and My Robot

In my pursuit of professional development in the past, I missed some goals and was less than successful in some areas. At the same time, I really wanted to succeed. So why didn't I? Here is what I learned.

Who is really in charge of me? Well, *I* am, aren't I? What I mean is, exactly what part of me is in charge? My first impulse is to say that it's my conscious mind, my conscious, thinking mind.

After all, *I* make decisions each day—waking at 6:00 a.m. and deciding to take a shower, deciding what to have for breakfast, deciding what to wear, deciding what to say in order to give a brilliant presentation to my staff, deciding which aspects of my marketing plan will be most effective, and so on. In fact, each day of my life *I* will make thousands of decisions that not only affect my own business life but the lives of many others. So it would certainly seem beneficial to know, for sure, who is really making all of these decisions. Let's use an example.

Say that I decide to give that brilliant presentation to my staff. Even though I *want* this presentation to be brilliant, somehow I procrastinate. Even though I *want* it to be successful, somehow I arrive late and unprepared. I try to put a good face on it, but as I am speaking I notice the distracted looks and the yawns once again.

I SEEM TO BE SABOTAGING MYSELF

What's happening? I seem to be sabotaging myself. So, once again, who is really making all my decisions? Who was the *I* that decided to procrastinate, to waste time and arrive late and pretend that I knew what I was talking about? And whoever that *I* is, he is obviously in conflict with the *I* that wants to succeed. Fortunately, I am in a position to find out what's going on. If I can find out, perhaps that will place me in a position to make better decisions, which in turn will create the kinds of actions that support my goals. Let's see.

I have discovered, over time, that there are two different, basic levels involved in my thinking process. One is my conscious thinking level. This involves all of the thinking and emotional feelings I am aware of, including all of my conscious decisions. I call this level of thinking the *judge* (you will see why in a few moments). Now one part of my judge acts as a collecting agency. It collects data from the environment, through my eyes, ears, nose, mouth and skin to help me decide how to move, how to react to information I perceive, how to avoid danger, etc.

A second function of the judge is that it makes rational decisions on what I will and won't do each day. And based on the factual input it receives, my judge decides what goals I can or can't achieve.

Okay, so far I know that what I call my judge, my conscious thinking mind, collects data and makes decisions based on that data. Now let's look a bit deeper into the situation.

I know there is much more to my mind, to my brain, than what I am aware of. For example, there is the autonomic nervous system that controls such bodily functions such as breathing, heart rate, temperature, circulation, digestion, involuntary muscle movements, and so on. All of these functions are subconscious—below my level of awareness. In addition to regulating bodily functions, I have learned that an additional function of my subconscious is to follow instructions based on previous input from the conscious mind, the *judge*. I call this subconscious function the *robot*, because it has no judging function. It simply follows instructions based on previous input from the conscious mind.

So with each conscious decision I make, my *robot* checks its memory banks for any meaningful associations of words, pictures, and emotions from the past that relate to the present decision. Those associations from my past are then transmitted from my robot to my judge, and I am motivated to action or inaction based on my previous performance. When I want to take a morning shower, get dressed and eat breakfast, my conscious judge decides to do so and my subconscious robot checks its memory banks and agrees with these decisions; after all, I have showered, eaten and gotten dressed successfully many times before. So I am able to proceed smoothly to do all of my morning routine without hesitation or stress. But when I want to have a successful presentation, if my previous ones were flops then my subconscious robot tells my conscious judge "I can't," and my conscious mind receives feelings of lack of confidence and motivation—with predictable results.

Unexamined, the judge/robot union might resemble a master/slave relationship, with the judge in charge. But in fact it is more complicated. While the judge may appear free to make a conscious decision, *it cannot create effective motivation until clearing it with the robot.* The robot checks its memory banks, which house the all-important memories of success and failure, and instantaneously relays data back to the judge for conscious action.

So what is actually controlling my success or lack of it? My success or failure in the present has been determined by what happened in the past. This is what is so important to understand: *Without some new kind of intervention, my success in the present is decided by my past, and images in my mind of past achievement, or lack of it, largely determine my behavior in the present.*

THE ROBOT FOLLOWS THE PAST

In fact, I, you, and all of us are governed by our subconscious memory banks of past experiences. But if the judge cannot act effectively without the consent of the robot, why call it the *judge?* We will see in a moment.

The next question is, to what extent are we locked into our previous performance? Can we change what is in our memory banks and, as a consequence, change what our robot tells our judge what we can or can't do?

Now my memories are all recorded in the form of words, pictures, and emotions; they accumulate with time and are non-erasable. Let me repeat that: recorded experiences from the past are non-erasable. But I can recall these words and pictures from the past. I can recall them on the conscious screen of my imagination. For example, I can project a past image of myself communicating with clients or giving a presentation.

But here is the exciting part. I can also project on my mental screen a self-image (my imagination) concerning every performance, talent, and characteristic I may possess. I can project that I am effective at communicating with people or I have poor communication skills; that I have no patience or I'm patient and understanding; that I'm a born winner or a born loser.

I AM CONTROLLED BY
THE MENTAL PICTURES I FORM

If, in my self-image, I cannot see myself achieving something, then my robot will tell my judge I cannot do it, and I literally will be unable to do it. So I must change my internal pictures before there can be a lasting behavior change in my emotions and my resulting performance. If I change my self-image, I change my personality. And if I change my personality, I change my behavior.

I said previously that my memories are non-erasable. I cannot remove the subconscious limits I have previously placed on myself, but I can set new limits within which I must live. In order to do this, I must trick my robot. And this is another very important point. I can trick it because *the robot is incapable of differentiating between a real success and a success that is repeatedly and vividly imagined in full detail.* This is not a quick fix. It takes work, and I have to learn a new skill. This new skill is called *simulation.*

So what have I learned thus far? Well, I have learned why I sometimes fail even though I want to succeed. I have learned that my conscious mind, my *judge,* is not in total control of my behavior, and that my subconscious mind. my *robot,* determines much of my behavior based on my past performance. And I have learned that it is possible to trick my *robot* into changing the negative pictures of my past. So at this point I am already in a more advantageous position than when I started. I am determined to pursue my professional development and to succeed in my goals. And to further this I am ready to learn how to achieve my goals by manipulating my robot.

Action Steps for this chapter:

1) Re-read this chapter several times, with intervals between each reading. The purpose of re-reading this material is not because you have forgotten it, it is to set a process in motion that I will be discussing more in the chapters ahead.

2

PRACTICAL SIMULATION
—A SELF-MANAGEMENT SKILL

When he was nine years old Stevie Cauthen placed a saddle on a bale of hay and pretended to ride it. His father disapproved of this foolishness and told him to put the saddle down and take the bale of hay to the barn. Stevie said, "Dad, I'm riding my thoroughbred—16.2 hands, and strong and fast." His dad replied, "Don't be ridiculous, son, go do your chores." But Stevie Cauthen went on to become the youngest Triple Crown winner in history, winning the Preakness, Kentucky Derby and Belmont Stakes. At the age of nine he had already mastered the science of sensory vision.

But before we look at sensory vision, let's return for a moment to what I know about myself. My conscious judge is not in total control of my behavior and my subconscious robot determines much of my behavior based on my past performance. So how can I manipulate my robot into changing the negative pictures of my past, or, like Stevie Cauthen, inventing new, positive pictures where there is no past experience?

The process is called *sensory vision,* or *simulation,* and it is a practice that all highly effective leaders engage in daily, whether they do it intentionally or not. By using sensory vision I employ my right-brain skills—they include imagination, intuition, creativity and spatial reasoning—to guide myself through a series of virtual reality scenarios. I exercise my imagination to visualize the achievement of my goals in sensory-rich images that include all the details of sight, sound, smell, taste and touch.

The effectiveness of this approach was first recognized in Olympic athletes who practiced mental as well as physical training. They were taught to visualize every detail of their successful future performances, employing all their senses and motor skills. It is now an integral part of athletic training. Let me give you an example. Do you remember Olympic Decathlon champion Bruce Jenner? Four years prior to his accomplishment he was in college in Eugene, Oregon. Each morning at breakfast time he would write on a piece of paper, "100 meters, 10.3 seconds; high jump, 6'3"; long jump, 23'6"; shot put, over 50 feet," and visualize himself doing just that. Four years later he won the Olympic Gold in the Decathlon by achieving those goals from within a tenth of a second to a quarter of an inch! Now I know that only two percent of people are familiar with this process, but this two percent constitutes the high-achieving individuals in all occupations. So I will begin emulating this two percent by using my imagination rather than my memory, and by so doing I will act like a highly successful CEO. I will begin reprogramming my subconscious robot for my business success.

But what if I have no past successes, no memory of real achievement? What if I want to achieve something today that I never achieved before? What do I do?

As you have already figured out, I use anticipation simulation. That is, I anticipate my future achievements by performing them successfully in my imagination. Now remember, the human nervous system cannot tell the difference between an actual experience and one vividly imagined. Vividness × imagination = reality in the subconscious mind. One of the most profound formulas I can memorize is $V \times I = R$.

So by imagining my experiences vividly and in detail, my subconscious robot records them, and my potentially successful activities of the future become new, permanent, simulated memories.

V × I = R

Once I have these simulated memories recorded, I can conjure them up again at will and replay them, just as I can imagine and replay events that actually occurred in the past. To be a highly-successful achiever, to be an effective leader, I must on a daily basis imagine and fantasize that person I would most like to become. I must imagine and fantasize those conditions that I would most like to create. For example, I can imagine tens of thousands and sometimes even millions of customers benefiting from my products and services.

These rich sensory images of achievement, when systematically programmed into my central nervous system, will literally begin to change the chemistry of my body; in turn, this will result in changes in my self-esteem, my self-confidence, my mood swings, my emotional drive and my ability to perform. (I'll describe more about this in the following chapters.).

The goals that Stevie Cauthen, Bruce Jenner and others have achieved are a result of imprinting the images of success into the right side of the brain. It is something like placing success on an autopilot; once successful images are recorded, the subconscious robot believes them to be real and directs the conscious mind and the body chemistry to reflect them. Winners simulate winning! This is also something I should memorize.

WINNERS SIMULATE WINNING

In talking about visual simulation I have mentioned the effectiveness of creating detailed images. Let me expand a bit on the idea of images. What I'm about to describe can seem silly...playing with pictures, but the effects are impressive. Mike Vance, the former Dean of Walt Disney

University, coined the term *picturization process*. This is how it works. I begin with my end result in mind and work backwards. I think of a goal I want to achieve and I then take a picture of it and make a goal poster/story board. For example, let's say I want to have a fine home. I'll start by taking some photos or cutting pictures out of a magazine; then I will add pictures of me either by using my computer or simply by pasting them on. The results are a picture of me in front of a three car garage, then another of me walking up to the front door of a beautiful home; next I'm in the living room looking out over the ocean, and then in the den looking out over the harbor with a view of my sailboat.

When I repeatedly look at the pictures of myself in my new home, they create imprints in the right side of my brain. Now remember the formula $V \times I = R$ (vividness × imagination = reality). Whatever I vividly imagine is recorded in my subconscious robot. As I'm viewing these pictures, my subconscious believes they are real. It then creates neurological pathways to change my self-image and my motivation, and I make daily decisions that move me in the direction of the simulation.

In the past, before practicing this, whatever goals I achieved were by chance; now I am doing it intentionally. When I control the images in my mind, I am actually controlling my actions as well. As William James said, "What you see is what you get!" Mental simulation is the closest thing to a wish-granting Fairy Godmother.

But what if a part of me denies all of this future success? How many times have I said to myself "I can't imagine doing that"? This declaration closes down the right side of the brain, the visionary side. Remember, I must change my internal pictures before there is lasting behavior change in my conscious emotions and my subsequent performance.

Here is an illustration from a seminar I presented for Coca-Cola. Gerry Graves, their former Vice President, had approximately 250 account managers and distributors in the hotel meeting hall. On the stage I had set up a raised plank approximately ten inches wide, about one foot above the floor. I asked for a volunteer to come up on the stage and walk across it. To give them some incentive I offered twenty-five dollars to anyone who would do it. Gerry accepted the challenge and easily walked across the plank, hardly giving it a thought.

I then described another challenge. I suggested widening the plank by another ten inches to a total of twenty inches to make it easier to walk on. But then I described extending it and suspending the plank between the John Hancock Tower and the Prudential Tower in Boston. I offered an incentive of $5,000 dollars and asked Gerry if he would take up this challenge. "No!" he responded emphatically.

I said, "What if I were to hold one of your account managers by his feet from the John Hancock Tower and if you didn't come across I'd drop him?"

"Depends on which one," he said jokingly.

"Your highest producer!" I tossed back.

Now why did he walk the plank in the hotel so easily? The reason is that his mind walked the plank and his body followed. He might have had many experiences in his childhood walking across planks or even railroad tracks of a similar width. So, without being aware of it, he had replayed his past or he had used anticipation simulation and pre-played himself walking the plank confidently and successfully, or both.

But what happened when I described the plank extending from tower to tower? The plank would have been wider and easier to walk than the narrow one in the hotel. However, there were additional factors added to the equation: he was afraid due to the height and his imagined fear of falling. And, in fact, with that frame of mind he would have been wise not to make the attempt because by imprinting a fall in his mind, neurological pathways would have been created that would likely cause him to fall. The body achieves what the mind has rehearsed. Gerry's mind would have to successfully walk the plank from tower to tower in order for his body to follow.

So what have I learned up to this point? Well, I've already learned that my conscious self, my judge, is not in complete control of my life, and that my judge has to clear things with my subconscious robot. And I know that my self-image, recorded and stored by my robot, can prevent me from achieving many of the things I want to do. But now I have learned I can trick my robot into believing a new reality by vividly imagining my successful achievements ($V \times I = R$) and replaying them frequently. I can help make the process more effective by creating physical pictures of my future success and imprinting them in my brain by simply viewing them.

There is really nothing difficult about doing these things. And they can literally change my life. If Stevie Cauthen and Bruce Jenner could do them, I can do them, too! Remember, winners simulate winning. And once I start this process, I set my autopilot, and thus my daily performance, on an automatic course toward achieving my goals.

Psychologists tell us that our more-or-less permanent self-image is typically formed by the age of twelve. Until now I may have been held back by that self-image, but now I no longer intend to let a twelve-year-old run my life!

Action Steps for this chapter:

1) Re-read this chapter several times, with intervals between each reading.

2) Begin practicing visual simulations. For example, in your mind's eye, picture yourself achieving a professional triumph. Do this with as much clarity and detail as you can. Imagine the award ceremony, promotion announcement or bonus payment; the acknowledgment of your

achievement by your peers; feel your own personal satis-faction at a job well done. When you have created a sim-ulation like this, practice recreating it in your mind sever-al times until the process feels comfortable.

3) Creating composite physical pictures may seem like child's play, but it is a powerful technique to direct you on a course toward achieving your goals. At this time, choose at least one goal you want to achieve and which can be shown pictorially. Locate or make several pictures that depict this goal and place pictures of yourself in these set-tings. Place the composite pictures in a place where you will view them frequently as part of your routine. Don't just glance at them casually. Take a few moments to look at them and allow their significance to sink in; that's *you* in the pictures, and that's the goal *you* will achieve!

3

PSYCHOLINGUISTICS PLUS —A SELF-MANAGEMENT SKILL

By now I'm beginning to feel good about all of this new knowledge. I am now convinced that *winners simulate winning,* and that the simulation must be *vividly imagined* for it to become *reality* in my subconscious robot (V × I = R). What makes me feel good is not only opening up the avenues to success, it's that I'm starting to feel like I'm more in control, that I can determine my own destiny to a larger degree than before. And with this in mind, I'm ready to explore the next phase that begins with a story.

There was a man in the supermarket with a 2-year-old child seated in his cart, obviously his son. The child was crying, wanting to go home. The father said, "Calm down, Harvey, it's okay. We'll be going home in a few minutes. We'll have something good to eat, we'll play games, watch Big Bird and Barney on TV. Relax, Harvey!" A woman in line behind him observed this and came over to compliment him on the patience he demonstrated and how nicely he was speaking to his son. With a smile the man replied, "I'm Harvey."

This is my way of introducing *psycholinguistics,* which is the science of the relationship between behavior and language. I want to employ this relationship in a deliberate way; and the way I want to do it is through positive *self-talk.*

While the right brain takes care of feelings and spatial visualization (and thus visual imagination), the left brain (verbal, analytical) can also play a powerful role in reprogramming my subconscious robot. Just as my performance in life is determined by my self-image, and my self-image can be changed by visual images, it can also be changed through self-talk. Here is a powerful example.

Dr. Emile Coue was a physician in France who cured many of the terminally ill patients he worked with. He would ask them a series of questions, such as "Do you love your family and want to continue to be with them? Is the life you are living of some worth? Do you want to live?" The patients all replied in the affirmative. He needed to develop a strong desire to live in his patients before he informed them of what they had to do.

Then Dr. Coue would say the following: "I'm going to give you eleven words to say tomorrow morning when you awaken, and if you say these words, it will increase the chances that you will live and they will help you to attain your lifetime goals. Will you say the eleven words?" Again they would all respond in the affirmative.

"Before I give you the words you must understand there are two stipulations. One, you must say the words aloud, and two, you must say them twenty times." These are the eleven words (translated to English). "Day by day in every way I'm getting better and better."

Then Dr. Coue would tell his patients: "Say these words daily, twenty times, and your situation in life will be improved *even if you don't believe what you're saying*."

But in fact, many of his patients did not say them because of the lack of discipline and/or the embarrassment with family members. Had I been present, maybe I would also have asked the patients, "Are you willing to say these words aloud even though they may embarrass you or seem foolish? Is the opportunity to live sufficient to overcome your embarrassment?"

Those patients who did recite the words daily as instructed created biochemical changes in their bodies that not only improved their physical condition but positively affected their self-image and overall confidence.

The fact is, words are powerful things that affect my behavior. So do I talk to myself? Yes! (My brother Ron says he likes to talk to himself because he likes talking with intelligent people.)

For example, what I say before a performance is as important as what I say during a performance. Before a performance, I always say, "I can see myself achieving that." Then I play the perfect visual execution in my imagination. When my performance is correct, I say, "That's like me; the next time I'll do the same thing." If my performance is poor, my self-talk is, "That's not like me; the next time I will do it correctly." Then I replay it over in my imagination correctly. In this way my self-talk predicts and perpetuates my performance in advance. It controls my emotions, causing a change in my behavior and performance.

Current research on the effect of words and images offers amazing evidence of the power that words, spoken at random, can have on body functions. Since biofeedback equipment shows that thoughts and speech can raise and lower body temperature, secrete hormones, relax muscles and nerve endings, dilate and constrict arteries, and raise and lower pulse rate, and since these functions have an effect on behavior, it is obvious that I can benefit by controlling the language I use on myself. I must feed my subconscious robot positive thoughts about myself and my performance. I must do this so methodically and vividly that my self-images change to conform to the new, higher standards that I am declaring.

Winners do this intentionally or naturally. They rarely put themselves down in actions or in words. Losers fall into the trap of saying, "I can't," "I'm a jerk," or "I can't do it." Winners use constructive feedback and self-talk every day: "I can," or "I look forward to," or in the case of failure "Next time I'll get it right." These conscious word thoughts create subconscious realities.

Unsuccessful people, on the other hand, victimize themselves with negative self-talk, worries and doubts. They find all sorts of reasons why their dreams can't come true. They convince themselves of their failures in advance.

I WILL REMAIN OR BECOME WHAT I BELIEVE MOST ABOUT MYSELF

If I believe I am an ineffective leader, then my self-talk statement should be, "I am a highly effective leader." If I believe I lack compassion when dealing with people, my statement should be, "I am compassionate when dealing with people." If I react defensively and/or inadequately to negative situations, I should say, "I enjoy responding positively and effectively to negative situations."

I use psycholinguistics in eating. My diet was poor fifteen years ago. My affirmation was, "I enjoy maintaining healthy eating habits." Doctors told me for years to drink more than one or two glasses of water per day. My affirmation was, "I find great pleasure in drinking several glasses of refreshing water daily." So who says people can't change? I have maintained healthy eating habits for over ten years now, and I drink a minimum of eighty ounces of water daily. We all can change.

Another example of the power of self-talk is golf champion Tiger Woods. At age twelve he would lie on his bed listening to a tape recording of himself saying, "I believe in myself. I am focused and determined. My will is my greatest asset. I am a champion." Did this work? Well, he was the first amateur to win three consecutive U.S. Amateur Championships. He was the youngest player to win the Masters (1997) by the largest margin of victory in the 20th Century, and the first Afro-American to win the Masters.

Behavioral psychology informs us that our behavior and feelings are related. If I act happy I will begin to feel happy. If I verbally express an emotion I feel the emotion, so outward behavior triggers inner feelings. It is why Tiger Wood's father said to him, "Your competition is not important, but your thoughts and emotions are!"

An example of how behavior triggers emotions is displayed by the employees at Walt Disney theme parks. If you are ever at a Disney park and have the opportunity, ask a sweeper, "How do you like being a sweeper, following horse drawn carriages and picking up manure?" Their response will be, "I'm not a sweeper. I'm an actor. I'm one of the cast members whose job it is to act like a sweeper." These employees are encouraged to play the roles of happy, dedicated, motivated employees. They act their way from roles into genuine feelings, and then from better self-images to more effective behavior. When I think, visualize, speak and act in a happy way, I feel happy. When I think, visualize, speak and act in a confident way, I become confident. When I think, visualize, speak and act in an enthusiastic way, I become enthusiastic. And when I think, visualize, speak and act like an effective leader, *I become an effective leader!*

WHEN I THINK, VISUALIZE, SPEAK AND ACT LIKE AN EFFECTIVE LEADER I BECOME AN EFFECTIVE LEADER!

Speaking of feelings and emotions, I'm going to invent a new word here—*emotionalize*. I need this word because it's my intention to deliberately introduce emotions into the process of professional development; that is, I'm going to *emotionalize!* Now when I do this, when I emotionalize my thoughts while doing visual simulations and self-talk, it has 100 times the impact of imprinting my goals on my subconscious memory banks, to change behavior and improve my performance.

Let me give an example. When John Kennedy was shot it was an extremely emotional time for me. As a consequence, the moment was strongly imprinted in my brain. I was in my high school typing class. Tony Chinappi was sitting next to me, and I had on a gray sweater my Mother had knitted. I could go on to tell many more details, but you get the point.

Now it is not just negative emotions that get strongly imprinted in our brains; strongly positive emotions do the same. And not only do we react positively to our own positive emotions, we react positively to those of others. To illustrate:

A pastor in a church wanted to get a raise. The Bishop was visiting one Sunday, and during his sermon the pastor was heard to remark dejectedly, "I am the pastor in this church and I earn $250 a week and this is not enough!"

The assistant pastor echoed his complaint, "I am the assistant pastor in this church and I earn $125 a week and this is not enough either!"

Then it was time for hymns, and the organist began playing so beautifully that the congregation began to sing with more gusto than usual. This so delighted the organist that he almost fell off his bench from the enthusiasm of his playing. Then the singing became so energetic, so filled with joy and fervor, that no one could remember having such a good time. With the last note of the last hymn ending, the organist suddenly leapt from his bench and sang, "I am the organist of this church and I earn $500 a week, and *there is no business like show business like no business I know!*"

There are two groups of people who are usually good at this emotional behavior. The first types are the extremely high achievers. Have you ever seen the intense emotions on the faces of players in the locker room before a Super Bowl Game? Or the intense expression on the face of a master musician who is so involved with the music that the outside world doesn't exist? The fact is that winners are extremely emotional, and very skilled at thinking, speaking, visualizing and acting positively.

Now every one of us is skilled at emotional simulation, whether or not we are aware of it. Every one of us sees ourselves in future scenes; every one of us talks about ourselves; and every one of us acts in a way that reinforces our self-images. The difference is that some of us do it positively, some indifferently, and some negatively.

I've already mentioned the first group of positive simulators, the high achievers. The second group of people who strongly emotionalize their simulations and self-talk are those who are discouraged and depressed. They see themselves as losing, feeling sad and lonely, and they articulate this by saying "I hate myself and my job," and "I can't see myself being happy." They say this in a highly emotional state, reinforcing this poor self-image. And why is this a fairly common phenomenon? Why do so many people have difficulty in emotionalizing the goals they want to achieve? Of course in some cases there are mental disturbances or unusual circumstances that prevent it, but I believe that for the majority it is either a lack of self-confidence or the result of bad habits, or both.

Here is a first clue that leads out of this dilemma, and it may at first seem counter-intuitive. I ask myself the question, am I happy because I'm productive, or am I productive because I'm happy? Think about it. The American philosopher William James put it this way: "We are happy because we sing, we don't sing because we are happy." In fact, psychologists tell us that it's happy people who are productive. (Productive people are happy but it's because they were happy first, before being productive!)

Here's an experiment. Try power walking, running or playing an active sport like basketball or tennis. In the midst of the action, try saying to yourself "I'm depressed, I'm depressed." You'll notice that it doesn't feel real, and you don't really feel depressed. It's hard to be down because actions trigger positive feelings.

So the message here is, *when you act it you become it.*

I can't begin to tell you how many times I have re-read this chapter. Yet each time I do I still feel a bit overwhelmed with the sheer power of information in it. In addition to positive visualizing, I'm now factoring in the art of positive self-talk. But not any kind of self-talk, because to make my self-talk most effective I need to *emotionalize* it; I really need to *feel* my future achievements! And one of the best ways to do that is to act out a role of success that alters my moods, my confidence, my self-image so that I start to *become* the person I've imagined. For those readers who enjoy a logical sequence (and who probably enjoy flow charts), here is a summary of how it works.

1) My left-brain (verbal) is programmed by positively stating what I want (most effective in the first person, present tense).
2) I intentionally see what I want in my imagination (right brain, visual).
3) To reinforce reprogramming of my right brain, I act as if I have achieved what I see in my imagination.
4) My acting out enables me to begin to *feel* the emotions associated with my self-talk and visualization.
5) As I feel the positive emotions, I will gradually *become* that person I imagined myself to be.
6) As I become the person I want to be, my performance will reflect it.

I SAY IT, SEE IT, ACT IT, FEEL IT, BECOME IT —AND DO IT!

How long does all of this take? The answer is easy; it takes from twenty seconds to twenty years, depending on your particular goals, your determination and how steadfast you are in using this process.

But it's not all hard work. When I utilize my personal simulations and self-talk, I do it with a feeling of playfulness. At the same time I am serious about the results because I know that *play and simulation are the most effective routes to learning and growth.*

From time to time in this book I ask myself, why do some people achieve almost impossible goals in the face of insurmountable odds? Why do some people constantly pull themselves back up and others give up and stay right where they are? Why do some people live lives that are full and rewarding while other people let the best in life pass right on by? What separates the winners in life from those whose lives are lived indifferently?

The answer is related to self-image. And I am modifying my self-image, recreating past successes and creating future ones through the intentional exercising of my imagination, self-talking and acting. I may not achieve perfection, but I am convinced I will attain excellence.

My personal development is the springboard to my professional excellence. This statement is so very important that I'm going to repeat it. *My personal development is the springboard to professional excellence.*

Action Steps for this chapter:

1) As your first step I'd like you to simply think about something. In this and the previous chapters, I've described a process that, while fairly simple, is not something most of us are used to doing. Except for problem solving or making practical decisions, where we use conscious volition, our minds are used to being passive and reactive. When we imagine something, it just "happens." When we think about ourselves, that, too, just "happens." We don't often formally and intentionally think about ourselves and we don't often formally and intentionally imagine our futures. But this is a whole new ball game. I'm now asking you to begin using your mind proactively. This means willing your mind to follow your commands. This is like exercising a muscle for the first time, and for most people it takes some getting used to. You don't have to

become an instant expert at this, but I'd just like you to be aware of it in this perspective.

2) A large amount of information has been packed into this short chapter. Please re-read it several times, with intervals between each reading.

3) Identify a few areas in which you believe your performance is inadequate, and write down affirmative statements for each of these areas. Example: "I enjoy business challenges and I take action in confronting and solving them." Or, "I make everyone I meet during the business day feel better about themselves and the company we work for." Or "I feel energized and vital, and that I have accomplished something worthwhile at the end of each business day." Make sure your statements are in the first person, present tense. Start a habit of reading your statements to yourself several times each day. Put some gusto into your statements—emotionalize them! If you don't believe them at this time, pretend! Remember, your subconscious robot doesn't care if you believe them or not, they will still begin the process of changing your life.

4) In small ways, each day, start to *act* as if you are already the person you want to be. This doesn't mean you should run out and buy an expensive car. Maybe it's something as subtle as your posture—the way you hold yourself. Maybe it's taking the time to dress in a way that presents you as more professional. Maybe it's being aware of how you greet people. Maybe it's the orderliness of your desk. From time to time, ask yourself: *how will I act differently as I gradually become the person I want to be?*

4

The Force of Habit
—A Self-Management Skill

At this point I have become empowered by the knowledge of a potent sequence. Because it is so important I'll repeat it again in large type.

SAY IT, SEE IT, ACT IT, FEEL IT, BECOME IT —AND DO IT!

On the face of it, it seems easy. I speak my goals, emphatically, emotionally, and in the present tense; I vividly visualize myself achieving them in my imagination; I act, where practical, as if I have already achieved them and, by so doing, I start to feel as if they are already realized; together, my speech, my visual imagination, my acting and my positive emotions all tell my subconscious robot to create new records of my success. Now, when I want to accomplish these goals, my robot says "Yes! They are do-able!"

Remember the example of the Coca-Cola vice president who easily walked across the short plank on-stage, but balked at walking across a long plank stretched between two skyscrapers in spite of a financial reward? His robot was telling him he could do it on-stage, but he would fall and kill himself if he attempted it up high.

When my robot says "I can!" it means that with my confidence and images of success I will begin doing the behaviors to reach my goals—I am on autopilot towards success. Yes, but...

But what? Well, for one, what about my existing habits? Like most of us, my mind is not used to being proactive. I have not been in the habit of vividly imaging what I want, let alone speaking it aloud and acting it out. So what is needed for me to sufficiently change my habits to adopt this new mode of proactive living?

Well, one thing that works beautifully is necessity. I'm thinking of a nature film I recently saw. Every morning in Africa a gazelle wakes up. It knows it must run faster than the fastest lion or it will be killed. Every morning a lion wakes up. It knows it must outrun and catch the slowest gazelle or it will starve to death. On the African plain, it doesn't matter whether you are a lion or a gazelle because when the sun comes up you'd better be running.

But changing my own habits is more subtle. I'm not in immediate danger of losing my life. This gives me room to forget, to procrastinate and to just simply ignore what my rational self wants to accomplish. Absent immediate necessity, habits are surprisingly tough things to change.

On the one hand I can change my behavior instantly. If I want to get up early and begin working on my sales presentation, all I have to do is will myself to do it. Right? Yes, don't I wish! Because on the other hand, my old habits are so ingrained that two difficult obstacles must be overcome. First, I must *remember* what my objective self wants to accomplish—for example, wanting to rise early and get some work done. Second, the part of me that wants to get this done *must overcome* the lazy part that wants to remain in bed. Both are absolutely necessary. If I forget about wanting to get up early, I won't even try; and if my lazy side wins and I stay in bed, then my rational side also loses.

Fortunately I have figured out what is going on and I have developed a routine that, if followed, ensures victory for my rational self—that is, for my long-term goals. And it doesn't start when I get up, it starts at night. I have found that there is a right way and wrong way to go to bed at night, and a right way and wrong way to get up in the morning. The worst thing I can do in the evening is to watch the 11:00 news. In fifteen minutes I'm likely to view some of the most criminal, violent, tragic events in the world. What kind of sense does that make? I want to have a restful sleep, and I have just programmed my mind with pictures of stress, anxiety and pain. Remember that the subconscious robot sees these things and believes them; the results from the news are imprints of an awful world filled with disaster, trauma and suffering. And although I have critical faculties that understand that these events on the news are not balanced, night after night my subconscious records these images and builds up a picture of a world in which nothing good can be accomplished.

So instead of watching the late night news, I spend thirty minutes listening to relaxing music, reading a favorite book, watching an uplifting TV show, or spending thirty minutes reading this book. Remember that if I put garbage in, I get garbage out. If I have positive thoughts, then I get positive results.

So now it is morning. I have just had a restful eight hours of sleep and my alarm goes off. Is that the first thing I want in the morning, to be alarmed? No! Do I have a radio alarm? Yes. That sounds fine until I wake up to the lyrics, "I can't live without you," or "You're no good, baby, you're no good." That first song heard in the morning is hummed all day, and its words create feelings in the body and mind. Is that how I want to be programmed for the day?

Instead I can engage in a *performance ritual* every morning—positive habits of behavior that will have a beneficial effect on my mind and body.

Now before I proceed, let's go back for a moment to the example of Dr. Coue telling his terminally ill patients to say, "Day by day in every way I'm getting better and better."

And you'll recall I added the hypothetical questions, "Are you willing to say these words aloud even though they may embarrass you or seem foolish? Is the opportunity to live sufficient to overcome your embarrassment?" Now I have to ask myself a similar question (although my life is not at stake, merely my success or failure). Am I willing to engage in activities that are very optimistic and positive even though at times they may seem naive, simplistic or empty? Do I strongly want to succeed in my goals? My answer is an unequivocal "yes."

Okay. Back to my morning performance ritual. Understand that I am not naturally a high-energy morning person. I used to wake up with an annoying alarm, drag myself out of bed and glumly wash-up and head for the coffee. But now I have gotten together with one of my best friends, and I have explained to him that I want to start my day with a confidence-building cassette tape or CD, based on what he thinks about my skills and character traits. We have discussed this and we have recorded him talking about me. On the tape he tells me that I am one of the most exciting presenters he has ever seen, that I have the capacity to inspire and uplift the lives of everyone I meet, and that he believes in my total integrity, my ability to reach my goals, etc.

The actual playback time is short, less than nine minutes. With an electrical timer that turns the power on, I arrange to be awakened every morning with his message. Wow! What a confidence-builder! What a way for me to begin a productive day. (Now remember that my subconscious robot hears this and believes it even if my conscious judge has doubts.

"GOOD MORNING. YOU ARE TERRIFIC!"

For the next part of my morning performance ritual, I jump out of bed and clap my hands several times. Seem silly? But this is a trigger mechanism to remind me that I am willing to do those activities and behaviors the average person does not want to engage in. Next I say to myself, "I feel happy, I feel healthy, I feel terrific. I'm looking forward to giving an outstanding presentation of my program to Corporation X. It's going to be another great day, and something wonderful is going to happen to me today!" I say all of this with great conviction, and I remind myself that what I think about with emotion, I start to become.

I then jump in the shower and the speaking ritual continues. I say to myself, "I would rather attempt to do something great and fail, than attempt nothing and succeed!" Then I repeat to myself, "Do it! Do it! Do it!" fifty times.

When I first began doing this I had to remind myself that this is what winners do naturally; and I also had to frequently remind myself that when asked if, in order to achieve my goals, would I be willing to say and do things that are very optimistic and positive, I answered "Yes!"

This routine also works by "faking it." For example, have you ever gone to bed at 2:00 a.m. and had to get up at 6:00 a.m. to present at 8:00 a.m.? You are anxious and restless all night and have had three or four hours sleep, and you wake up with a head the size of a watermelon. What can you do? Here's what I do.

I trick my subconscious robot. When I feel bad I jump out of bed and scream, "I can fake it until I make it!" And I begin faking it by saying "I feel happy, I feel healthy and I feel terrific!" I see myself as feeling fit and ready. And I keep faking it until I *am* making it, because my subconscious robot reacts by feeding signals of winning behavior to my body, which makes me begin feeling better, and I end up giving a dynamite presentation. Remember the sequence, *I say it, see it, act it, feel it, become it—and do it!* My performance is largely determined by my self-image; my self-image is formed in my imagination through the repetition of positive simulations and self-talk statements.

Habits are the key. It isn't lack of skill or talent or intelligence or knowledge that prevents most people from realizing their dreams—it's poor habits. I know that *the main difference between those who have failed and those who have succeeded lies in the difference of their habits.* Good habits are the path to my success. The first rule I must live by is that I will form these good habits of feeding my subconscious robot healthy, positive, uplifting thoughts and pictures daily.

What I have done is to create rituals that program my brain for consistent winning. Must I employ the very same rituals every day, all the time? No, I can vary them. Must everyone use these particular rituals? No, each individual can design his or her own that are comfortable and work best. From the examples I have given here, you can probably devise some of your own that I have never even thought of.

Remember from the previous chapters that negative images, already recorded in your subconscious robot, powerfully affect your present-day performance. These negative images can't be erased—whatever gets recorded in the subconscious stays there—but they can be overwritten. That is, new, positive images can become the dominant ones. But this will only occur if you develop the right kinds of habits that feed your brain with healthy, positive, uplifting thoughts.

The single most important key to your success is to take control of your thoughts. Whatever you'd like to change or accomplish in your life, like increasing your income, improving your leadership skills, learning to let go of worries and relax, etc., you first must learn how to talk to yourself. That is the most important step you can take to actually achieving what you want. Winning is telling yourself over and over again with words, pictures and emotions that you are succeeding already, and acting the part.

SAY IT, SEE IT, ACT IT, FEEL IT, BECOME IT —AND DO IT!

Remember, unsuccessful people victimize themselves with negative self-talk and negative self-think. You are no longer in this category. As a success-oriented person you will now begin to habitually use positive self-talk. You will repeatedly tell yourself what you truly want to become. You will form a clear mental picture of what you want to achieve. And you will be on the path toward achieving it.

Habits are routines and rituals that become ingrained and are largely automatic. We do them without thinking. In this chapter I've described some proactive rituals that, in time, will become ingrained, positive habits. Nevertheless, we are not yet home free. Many old, ingrained, negative habits will hang on tenaciously.

In the next chapters we'll survey some of the science regarding the breaking of old habits and the installation of new ones, and I'll describe a system that reinforces good habits, one that really works!

Action Steps for this chapter:

1) Re-read this chapter several times, with intervals between each reading. This is not because you can't remember the material, which is fairly simple, it is to program your subconscious robot by feeding it relentlessly again and again!

2) Take an objective look at your nighttime activities before going to bed, and determine what kinds of impressions they make on your subconscious robot. Which of your activities need changing? Can you devise a nighttime routine that enables positive programming and with which you are comfortable? I recommend you write it down and keep it handy as a reminder. This takes a bit of thought. Are you willing to do it in order to succeed? Okay, then don't just read this—DO IT!

3) Similarly, look objectively at how you wake up in the morning, and the rest of your morning activities. Which of your morning activities need changing? Can you devise a

morning routine that enables positive programming and with which you are comfortable? Are you willing to do this in order to succeed? Then DO IT!

4) Everyone has occasional bad mornings. *Before* this happens, write down a series of things you will say and do to "fake it" when it *does* happen. Keep this in a handy place for when it is needed.

5) After completing the above, take a moment to realize you are engaged in a profound exercise, proactively changing your habits. Pat yourself on the back. You are on *The Proactive Path*. Congratulations!

5

REPETITION, FOCUS AND DISCIPLINE —SELF-MANAGEMENT SKILLS

Okay, I have now created some rituals, or exercises—positive habits—that will reprogram my subconscious robot and keep me on track for success. All well and good, but will I actually use them?

The majority of people who attend my seminars, watch my CD-ROMs or listen to my CDs agree enthusiastically that these exercises are beneficial. After a seminar they'll say, "This is great. I'm going to do it when I get home." Or "I will definitely begin it Monday morning before I go to work." And they are sincere. They have all the good intentions in the world. But what happens when they get home? The dog has made mud tracks all over the carpet, the kids need to be driven to music lessons, cousin Ralph calls and needs to talk, and there is that business report that is due in a few days.

And then there's actually remembering to do it. Which reminds me of the story of two teenagers about to flunk their music class. To be eligible to play in their championship game they have to pass a music appreciation course. Their teacher puts both in a room and has them listen to "Old McDonald" twenty times over. Then it's time for the exam, and there is only one question to fill in. It reads: "Old McDonald had a _____." The first teen looks at the question and says, "I don't know." The other says,

"It's 'farm' but I don't know how to spell it." The first teen looks smug and says, "I do: E-I-E-I-O."

Most of us are not that bad at remembering things, but nevertheless we all tend to become distracted and we all tend to forget the things that don't demand immediate attention. Out of sight, out of mind.

So two main obstacles to actually doing self-development exercises are distractions and forgetfulness. And then there are other considerations. How much time each day do I need to spend on these exercises, and how often should I do them? If I feel like doing them one day and not another, can I pack a bunch into one time and then skip doing them for a while? Let's see.

Repetition

We all know from our own experience that repetition imprints words and phrases in our memory. For example, like the two teenagers were asked to do in the story above, let's fill in the lyrics.

"Rudolph, the red-nosed - - - - - - - -"
"On top of old Smoky all covered with - - - -"
"Oh my darling, oh my darling, oh my darling - - - - - - - - - -"

(Just in case these aren't obvious, the answers are at the end of this chapter.)

Why do you remember the lyrics to these songs? Obviously, because you've heard them over and over for years. Now let's go a step further. Advertisers have spent large sums researching what types of ads are permanently imprinted in our subconscious, their most effective duration, the number of times they should be watched and heard, and how often they should be aired. One of the most important things they have learned is that spaced repetition of ads can change people's behavior in terms of product purchases. Do we remember ads that have aired at intervals, over and over again? You bet we do! Recognize any of these?

"Please don't squeeze the *Charmin*."
"*Trix* are for kids!"
"*Coke* is the real thing."
"Got *milk*?"

There are many advertisements I have not heard for years, but I remember them immediately because they were imprinted in me through the repetition of watching and hearing ads on TV or radio. It sounds simplistic, but it obviously works. A 30 or 60 second advertisement on TV or radio can change people's purchasing habits on products ranging anywhere from five dollars to fifty thousand dollars.

Another example. I know someone who has created a very successful mail order business. When he told me one of the secrets of his success it really surprised me. Like most of us mail-order amateurs, I had assumed that all you have to do is mail an effective promotional piece once or twice to the same person, and wait for the sales to come in. But he told me that for his product he needed to mail the same, or similar, promotional pieces at least six times to each person before he would get positive responses, and that sometimes it required ten mailings. Ten mailings to each person! Not only that, but the interval between mailings was critical. Too little time between mailings and the customers just got annoyed; too much time between mailings and the imprint on customers' minds diminished. It took that much well-timed repetition before those potential customers were motivated to buy!

Now, back to the prospect of imprinting positive changes into our subconscious robots. Have some of my important phrases taken root?

WINNERS SIMULATE WINNING

V × I = R (VIVIDNESS × IMAGINATION = REALITY)

SAY IT, SEE IT, ACT IT, FEEL IT, BECOME IT, DO IT!

Maybe not, because you haven't yet experienced enough repetition of these phrases. But if you read them each day for, say, a month, you'll never forget them. Regular, spaced repetition is the most effective basis for imprinting positive changes into our subconscious robots. So I know that if I want to effect permanent, positive changes in my behavior, and avoid *out of sight, out of mind,* I need a disciplined, daily support system.

Yet I am a busy person, you are a busy person, we are all busy people. So I won't ask myself, or you, to devote large amounts of time to self-development. After many years of trial and error, first on myself and then testing it with thousands of others, I have learned that the most effective compromise is what I call CPI3030. The CPI stands for *Continuous Performance Improvement,* and by continuous I mean on a regular, daily basis. The first *30* is for thirty minutes a day. The second *30* is for thirty days. Here is why this is so important.

Dr. Maxwell Maltz wrote the classic book, *Psychocybernetics,* dealing with self-image behavioral modification; that is, how to develop new habit patterns. He found (and other psychologists agree) that in order for any of us to change our behavior permanently and improve our self-images, we need to engage in a new behavior for 21-28 days consecutively. To be on the safe side, let's say 30 days consecutively.

So now I need to develop a new habit, the habit of reviewing the material in this book and doing the mental simulations for 30 minutes daily, because if it's out of sight, then it is out of mind. By following the instructions in this book and simulating the achievement of my goals and the rewards of my success daily, my actions will be a result of what my mind has rehearsed. And if I am a beginner, I need to do this for at least 30 days in order to make the changes permanent and to confirm that this system really works.

CONTINUOUS PERFORMANCE IMPROVEMENT: CPI3030

For me this system and this book now constitute my working notes. I read it daily and do the simulations for at least 30 minutes a day. If I do this, what effect will it have on my self-image and, as a consequence, on my actions? I know from my own experience, and that of thousands of others who have done it, that it will imprint new images on my subconscious robot and I will have the self-image (and the consequent motivation) to take positive action to achieve my goals. It's the Law of the Harvest: I reap what I sow. I will enjoy a successful harvest when I cultivate the mental skills, habits, and human qualities of highly effective people, and perform them daily. CPI3030 is a *do-it-to-myself* behavior modification system.

Now, ideally, for how many minutes should I do this each day? I have many enthusiastic students who, for example, spend 1-2 hours a day listening to my tapes while driving to and from their jobs. It is not necessary to do this, but I don't discourage them if they find it enjoyable. But it's spaced repetition that is most effective. Reading (or listening) for 30 minutes in the morning and 30 minutes in the evening is more effective than longer periods at one time. Even worse would be reading for 3 hours today and not reading/listening until 3 days later. Regular repetition is the key, not duration.

Focus
I'd like to recall a scene from the popular movie, *The Karate Kid*. In it, the boy, Daniel, is in a martial arts competition against a much bigger and stronger opponent, a bully who kicks Daniel illegally and hurts him badly. Daniel is down, the confidence drains from his face and his teacher, Mr. Miagi, must come out to the mat to help him. Even though he has trained for months, honing his skill and concentration, Daniel now says, "I want to quit and go home." Mr. Miagi slams his fist against the mat to get his student's attention and says, "The karate inside you. Let it out, Daniel-san. You must *focus!*"

Although in pain, Daniel begins to concentrate on a unique move he has practiced for months. For this move he must assume the posture of a graceful sea bird, his arms outstretched like great wings, standing on one leg with the other cocked tightly beneath him. The posture looks benign and harmless, and Daniel seems completely relaxed. His gaze is clear and unworried. No one understands what he is doing. The sneering bully, the shouting crowd, the championship match have all disappeared; there is only the concentration on visualizing his upcoming move. In his mind, Daniel has become the bird.

The match resumes. The bully rushes forward, eager to end it with a brutal finishing blow. Suddenly, Daniel uncocks his bent leg and executes his kick move with speed, grace and precision, totally surprising and completely disabling the bully. The judges and the crowd are stunned. No one except Mr. Miagi has ever seen a move like this—beautiful yet devastating. Daniel has won the match. He has focused his imagination so totally that his body obeyed. But even more important, he has regained his self-image, the image of a winner. *Winners simulate winning!*

From time to time we all find ourselves in difficult situations. Any time I'm in trouble or I feel I'm not being effective, I also go back to the basics. I go back to my simulations and self-talk statements that I am rehearsing in my imagination. I find it helpful to use a reminder phrase which I call *Focus 2*. It reminds me that first I need to focus on the goals I want to achieve, then I need to focus on the rewards I will receive from my success.

In relating this story from *The Karate Kid* I mentioned that Daniel seemed completely relaxed before he ended the match with a winning move. That, too, is an important component of focusing effectively. The process of imprinting our subconscious robots with new, positive images is affected by our moods. If I am not relaxed and in a secure place such as my home, study, office or car, my reading this material and doing the simulations will have less benefit. The pathway to my subconscious is opened by relaxation.

In fact, there is a special kind of relaxation that most widely opens the pathway to the subconscious. You can learn it in just a few moments. It is called *restful alertness*. Here's an example of how it works. Imagine you are strolling through a forest that is completely silent. Suddenly you hear the beautiful, striking call of a bird. Then the forest is silent once again. You stop and listen...and wait for the call to repeat.

Now use your imagination right now for a moment, close your eyes and place yourself in this situation. Imagine the silent forest. Hear the sudden call of the bird. Will it be repeated? Feel your calm alertness as you wait, with complete openness, to see if it will occur again. Notice that your mind is very quiet as you wait for the sound.

This is the state of restful alertness, and this state of mind is a simple yet powerful way for me to begin my daily exercises of visualizing and self-talk.

Discipline and Mental Rehearsal

Sometimes when I think it is too difficult to maintain the tenacity necessary to perform my daily reading and exercises, I remember the experience of Major Gerry Nesmeth, an Air Force pilot during the Viet Nam War. On February 3, 1966, he was shot down and landed in the China Sea. He was captured and spent seven years incarcerated in a 6 foot × 9 foot cement cell. For four years he didn't see another human being, experiencing solitary confinement in a pitch-black cell. Fed a plate of rice and one cup of water daily, he became completely emaciated. He lost 60 pounds over this time.

What would someone else have done in his situation? Become depressed? Feel terribly alone? Be consumed by anger? Be resentful of the folks back home? Or give up and just slowly die?

In spite of his weakness from lack of decent food, Major Nesmeth forced himself to do 200 sit-ups and 100 push-ups each day to maintain his physical and mental health. Before his imprisonment Major Nesmeth was shooting a golf game in the high 90s. To maintain his sanity he decided to play an imaginary round of golf each day during his seven years as a POW in North Vietnam. In his mind's eye he would walk up to the first tee and notice the wind blowing through the trees, enjoy the white fluffy cumulus clouds overhead, look to the rough on the right, then to the left. He looked down the fairway and saw the traps, but most importantly he saw the flag and hole. In his imagination he would take a few practice swings, then it was time to get down to business. His left arm was straight, his head was down, and he swung his powerful wood to drive the ball 260 to 290 yards. Then he would walk down the fairway for his second shot.

Major Nesmeth played four hours of golf a day, shooting par every day for seven years. After he was released, and only two weeks later, he played golf at the Augusta Nationals with PGA professional Orville Moody. *He shot a 74!*

A news reporter came running up to him and said, "Beginner's re-entry luck!"

The Major said, "Luck, heck. I haven't missed a par in seven years."

"What are you talking about? There are no golf courses in prison."

The Major replied, "There's a golf course in everyone's mind."

An amazing story, isn't it? And while this story is quite exceptional, it points to a truth common to all winners. When they don't have the opportunity to practice in actuality, they practice through simulation.

Major Nesmeth's persistence was duplicated, to one extent or another, by many other POWs. Several of them made guitars out of wooden sticks and strings. Although their crude instruments made no sound at all, those who knew how to play practiced from memory, listening in their imaginations. They taught each other many new chords, finger positions and songs. Some, who had never held a guitar before, are now accomplished guitarists!

Physical fitness abounded in the prison camps. When there was nothing else to do, they did sit-ups. One POW now holds the world's record—4,500 without resting!

I remember the iron discipline demonstrated by these men by coining a phrase: *do within when I am without.* This is an important reminder for me, so I'm going to print it in large type right here.

DO WITHIN WHEN I AM WITHOUT

When winners are without the means to practice in actuality, they work and practice in their minds to toughen themselves to the task. Some do it knowing the imagination is the greatest tool in the universe, and some do it naturally, spontaneously, unaware of what they are doing—one way or another, all winners do it! But most of us simulate haphazardly, often negatively, not realizing the effects of what we are doing. My objective is to remind myself of the process and then to do it deliberately, intentionally, in a directed way, every day. With all the goals I achieve, I must achieve them twice. I first simulate the achievement, and second, I actually achieve the goal in reality.

If a prisoner of war can do it for four hours a day for seven years in very difficult circumstances, can I do it for 30 minutes a day, every day...even if sometimes inconvenient? Setting aside 30 minutes as a regular, daily routine will help me in two ways: it will help me remember to do it, and with a regular time set aside for these self-development exercises I will be less tempted by distractions and interruptions.

All right! Now I know that spaced repetition is the effective way to perform positive simulations. I have determined that 30 minutes each day is a reasonable, do-able amount of time that will move me toward achieving my professional goals; and I know that a beginner must re-read this book and do the simulations for 30 days continuously for the simulations to permanently imprint on the subconscious robot (CPI3030). I've learned that the exercises are most effective when I am in a very relaxed, alert state of mind, and now I know how to get into that state of mind. From the examples given in this chapter I know that I can mentally rehearse future events and prep myself to succeed.

Besides all of this, an interesting thing is happening to me. The more I get into the habit of doing these exercises regularly, the more I am beginning to feel like a champion, a winner. As a youth I was not a high-energy, motivated person. But now I have begun to tap the Olympian within, and I am entering the "zone." I am developing the iron will of a champion! And it feels great!

When you get past the concepts and you, too, begin to experience this feeling, I believe you'll say, like I did, "Fantastic! It feels great!"

Words for blank spaces: reindeer, snow, Clementine

Action Steps for this chapter:

1) Re-read this chapter several times, with intervals between each reading. This is not because you can't remember the material, which is fairly simple, it is to program your subconscious robot by feeding the words to it again and again.

2) How badly do you really want to succeed? Can you make a firm commitment at this time to re-read this book and do the simulation exercises for 30 minutes a day, for

30 days? I hope so. If not, are you at least willing to start? Good!

3) Do the simple, restful alertness exercise (or any relaxation procedure you prefer) before starting your simulations.

4) Write down one or more specific goals you want to achieve. These may change as you continue, and that's okay; this is just a start.

5) For each goal you have written, practice visualizing yourself succeeding in that specific situation.

6) For each goal you have written, practice positive self-talk—and put lots of emotion behind it!

6

THE EM*BODY*MENT OF SUCCESS

If a prisoner of war can do simulations for hours each day for seven years in very difficult circumstances, can I manage to do it in comfortable surroundings for 30 minutes a day? At this point I have not made an iron-clad, long-term commitment, but at least for now I am doing it! And from the action steps of the previous chapter, I am finding the state of restful alertness to be very pleasant. I have written down my goals, visualized them, talked to myself about them, and imagined myself achieving them. Now I am starting to feel a bit more confident that this process is different from other self-development schemes; it appears to be something that really works.

It has been a bit new and strange, using my mind proactively like this—I mean doing intentional simulations—but little by little it is getting easier and more natural, and I am gradually beginning to feel that I am going to be a winner—no, wait, I should act like I am *already* a winner. I *am* a winner! I have a winner's attitude. And speaking of it, here's something that confirms the importance of attitude.

"What are the contributing factors that are most responsible for one's accomplishments, promotions and financial success?" The Carnegie Institute of Technology did a research study on this topic with 1500 engineers. Dr. David McClelland, while a professor at Harvard University, did a similar study in Cambridge, MA, that covered a period of twenty-five years. The results of both studies were very similar. They are surprising, even for engineers for whom we would suppose that technical knowledge is dominant.

Fifteen percent of success is due to one's aptitude, talent, and ability; eighty-five percent is due to skills in *human* engineering! Let me digest that. Knowledge of my field, what I have learned about presenting, my sales ability, my organizational skills; what you might call my technical job competence—all of these together count for only fifteen percent of my success! And the eighty-five percent from human engineering skills? Well, that would include motivation, ethical standards, adaptability, responsibility, honesty, communication skills, personal relationship skills, team player skills, and being a visionary.

So winning and excellence are primarily a result of personal and people skills. Now natural-born winners are good at personal and people skills but most of us, myself included, have had to learn them. And psychologists tell us that how well we learn them and use them is largely determined by the extent to which we have a *positive attitude*. These are such important points to remember that I want to repeat them here.

WINNING AND EXCELLENCE ARE MOSTLY DUE TO PERSONAL AND PEOPLE SKILLS

PERSONAL AND PEOPLE SKILLS DEPEND ON A POSITIVE ATTITUDE

Now I could spend a lifetime trying to understand all of the factors that come together to create a positive attitude, but I do know some of them and by now so do you. We know that the progression of positive speaking, positive visualizing and positive acting leads to positive feelings. (Remember? *Say it, see it act it, feel it, become it, do it!*) So I can say that positive thoughts and thought-pictures lead to positive feelings. And positive feelings, taken together, constitute a positive attitude. So one of the ways to cultivate a positive attitude is by doing the self-talk and visual simulations I have already described in some detail.

Now I'm the type of person who likes to know *how* things work. I know the "say it, act it, feel it..." sequence works, but *why* does it work? Incidentally, before I go any further I'm going to use an acronym for the "say it, act it, feel it..." progression—I'm going to call it *SSAFBD*. This will make it easier to repeat and will also help me to remember the sequence. (If you're like me, the first time you look at SSAFBD you'll try to verify what each letter stands for.)

So, once again, how does SSAFBD actually work? I mean, what's actually going on in my brain and in the rest of my body? Well, it is a fact that certain thoughts actually change my brain and blood chemistry to make me a better or worse performer.

Bio-behavioral scientists, endocrinologists and biochemists tell me that my self-talk and simulations control my emotions by stimulating the release of certain neurochemicals in my brain. As I'm thinking at this very moment, I'm generating new chemicals. When I think, my cells speak to each other through chemical messengers, and the chemistry of billions of cells throughout my body will change in response to what I imagine. When I produce positive images through simulations and self-talk, specific neuro-transmitters called *enkaphalins/beta endorphins* are released. In fact, I am releasing 60 neuro-transmitters that are 195 times more potent in their effect on body chemistry than morphine. The chemistry of billions of cells throughout my body will change in response to what I imagine. Each mental image or verbal declaration has a corresponding internal chemical state, and I can move from state to state by invoking the proper images and declarations. The effect of releasing these particular chemicals from the limbic gland of my brain, which is the seat of human emotions, and the limbic gland determines how I am feeling.

When enkaphalins/beta endorphins are released, I subjectively feel this by an enhanced mental alertness, greater motivation and confidence, increased persistence and higher levels of energy. My stress level is reduced, and I become better at problem solving, calmer in managing challenges. In essence, when my attitude is right, I feel like an effective leader—and a winner!

The body chemistry of pessimists is quite different. We sometimes associate pessimism with intellect; that is, we tend to believe that people who are overly critical are also more analytical and intellectual. But in fact science has shown that the opposite is really true. When I create negative visualizations and negative self-talk, my body secretes more hormones called gluttaglicoids or cortisol, which lessen the activity of my left-brain, the logical side. This inhibits the thinking process (and also causes a loss of short-term memory). While this knowledge hasn't yet filtered down to general awareness in the public, the fact is that optimists have more of their intellectual capacity available than do pessimists.

Also, optimists live longer than pessimists. Chronic and terminal illnesses are three times higher among pessimists after age forty-five.

OPTIMISTS HAVE MORE BRAIN CAPACITY THAN PESSIMISTS AND OPTIMISTS LIVE LONGER

I've read about *psychosomatic medicine,* which studies how the mind influences the body. The principle is that many diseases are not caused by germs. Everyone has germs, but only a few people get sick. Thus, many diseases are closely related to one's reaction to life. Dr. Bernie Siegel says, "99% of all illnesses are emotionally induced." Dr. Benson at Harvard Medical Center says, "Our thought process leads to good health or disease. A negative emotional state, such as anger, depression, pessimism, fear, self-doubt, worries, and stresses are associated with illnesses and minimal quality standards. These thoughts weaken my immune system; I become vulnerable to disease and culminate into frequent sickness, accidents, lower productivity, and early death. Anger is manifested in the body as uneasy cells, or dis-easy cells or diseased cells later on in life."

So my attitudes and emotions act as catalysts that have an effect on my body's immune system. I have a listening and thinking immune system that responds to the emotions associated with my pictures and self-talk statements. Therefore, emotional changes precede and cause physiological changes in my body. All of this medical data helps support what I am doing with SSAFBD.

The next thing that occurs to me is that the more of my waking hours are spent being optimistic, the more I will charge my success mechanism. How can I do this? One way is to stimulate my sense of humor. And speaking of a sense of humor, I'm going to test mine right now; you can take the test too. The following are a series of jokes. There will be a correlation between how I (and you) react to them and how successful I (and you) will be as a result. Let's score each of the following very simply, as "ha-ha" or "ugh," meaning funny or not. Smiles, chuckles and groaners count as funny. "Yuck" counts as "not." Ready? Here we go.

NOTE: IF YOU ARE ANNOYED, BORED OR OTHERWISE PUT OFF BY THE FOLLOWING, PLEASE CONTINUE READING—THERE'S SOMETHING IMPORTANT I WANT TO TELL YOU.

1) I asked Tony if my turn signal blinker in my car worked. He said yes-no, yes-no, yes-no, yes-no, yes-no, yes-no...

2) Why won't melons run away to get married in Las Vegas? They cantaloupe.

3) A man walks into a tavern and notices he's the only one there, apart from the barkeep, who's on the phone. The barkeep signals him that he'll be with him in a minute. The

man nods and bellies up to the bar to wait. Suddenly, he hears a little voice say, "Hey, you're looking pretty sharp today. New suit?" The man looks around but can't see anyone else nearby. Again he hears the voice, "That is a fabulous tie, chum." The man looks around again and still doesn't see anyone. "Hello?" he asks. "Is someone speaking to me?"

"You bet! I just had to say you look like a million bucks. Have you lost weight?"

A bunch of other tiny voices suddenly rise in agreement. The man realizes now that these voices are coming from a bowl of beer nuts on the bar in front of him. He stares at them as the barkeep finally hangs up and comes to serve his customer.

"What'll you have?" asks the barkeep.

"What?...oh, a pint of ale, I guess," mutters the man, still staring at the nuts. He finally looks up at the barkeep drawing his pint. "What's the deal with these nuts?" he asks.

The barkeep brings the man's pint over and sets it before him. "Oh, the nuts? They're complimentary."

4) Two boll weevils grew up in South Carolina. One went to Hollywood and became a famous actor. The other stayed behind in the cotton fields and never amounted to much. The second one, naturally, became known as the lesser of two weevils.

5) A man went into a hardware store to buy a chain saw. "I want a good one," he said. "One that'll cut at least ten trees per hour."

"Okay," the hardware store clerk said, "this model will easily do that."

The man took it home and came back to the hardware store the next day. "Dang," he said, "I used this for an hour and I was only able to cut down one small sapling!"

"Let me check it out for you," said the clerk, and he started up the chain saw.

"What's that noise?" asked the man.

6) Or have you seen these actual classified ads that appeared in print?

Dog for sale: eats anything and is fond of children.

Apartment wanted. Man, honest, will take anything.

We will oil your sewing machine and adjust tension in your home for $10.00.

7) Or these actual signs?

On a maternity room door: "Push, Push, Push."

On a physicist's door: "Gone Fission"

In a podiatrist's window: "Time Wounds All Heels."

Outside a muffler shop: "No appointment necessary. We'll hear you coming."

In a veterinarian's waiting room: "Be back in 5 minutes. Sit! Stay!"

On a utility company counter: "We'll be delighted if you send in your payment on time. However, if you don't, you will be."

8) Horse walks into a bar. Bartender looks at him and asks, "Why the long face?"

And the last one:

9) Pirate enters a bar. Has a peg leg, a hook on one hand and an eye patch. Sympathetic man asks him, "How'd ya get your peg leg?"

Pirate answers "Oh, 'twas in a bloody battle, got cleaved with a sword, cut my leg clean off."

Other man pauses, then asks "How about that hook on your hand?"

"Oh, 'twas a dagger blade...right through my wrist."

Another pause. Then, "Well, what happened to your eye?"

The pirate replies, "Seagull poop."

"Seagull poop?"

"Yep. Looked up at a passing seagull. Got it right in the eye."

"How could seagull poop make you lose your eye?"

"Wiped it with my hook."

NOTE

This test is deliberately misleading. You see, what's important is not the number of jokes or stories you find funny or unfunny, it's how you react to the ones you feel are not funny. Are you tolerant and empathetic enough to understand that it's okay for others to find humor where you don't? Can you encounter humor that you don't care for without becoming negative about it? The ability to tolerate and even appreciate things you don't agree with has a definite correlation with success. For those readers who are turned off by humor they don't like and stop reading at this point, this is often an excuse to grasp at something that will avoid bettering their own personal/professional lives. Failure needs excuses; success needs none.

Dr. Bernie Siegel, the well-known lecturer and author of *Love, Medicine and Miracles,* and countless other wonderful books on healing, says "...laughter is the pulse of life. A good laugh exercises the total body and releases hormones throughout the bloodstream. Laughing is like an aerobic workout."

I recently learned that there are 1000 laughing clubs in India. People get together weekly to tell each other jokes and to laugh. At one of the clubs, after several weeks no one had any new jokes to tell. What do you think they did? They thought that was pretty funny, so they laughed and laughed and laughed.

Laughter is great stuff, and it has helped me get through some difficult times in my life. For right now, one of the ways I maintain a positive, healthy attitude all day long is to be appreciative of humor wherever I see it, wherever I hear it, wherever it comes from. And it is certainly an enjoyable way to keep my endorphins plentiful.

Maintaining a positive attitude certainly isn't always easy. Just like everyone else, I find it hard to be optimistic when faced with tragic circumstances. What do highly effective leaders do in these circumstances? As I've already mentioned, either they are endowed with the natural ability to create positive thoughts in the face of negative events, or they are able to intentionally create them in spite of the bad circumstances. Personally, I fall into the latter category. I've had to learn how to do positive simulations. But in addition to the effectiveness of the simulations there is another benefit—the bleed-over effect.

When recordings of good times, or simulated good times, are imprinted onto my subconscious robot, the result is the release of beneficial chemicals. When these beneficial chemicals are released, their effect is not just temporary; it lasts and helps mitigate negative thoughts and feelings when they do come. It's the regular, simulated recordings of good times that secrete the endorphins that help to keep me going through the bad times.

Of course it takes determination, discipline and persistence to do this. I'm helped by remembering all of the winners I've known or read about. Winners such as Major Nesmeth, the POW who preplayed champion-level golf in his mind while incarcerated for seven years; young Stevie Cauthen, who visualized his marvelous future career as a jockey; or the deliberate and detailed visualizations of Bruce Jenner, who planned his every Olympic move in his mind and then actualized them.

Look at the choice I have. I can live a negative, depressed life, thinking about problems constantly, or I can live a positive, optimistic life, thinking about solutions. I may lose a job, I may hurt myself physically, I may get divorced, I may experience the death of a loved one, I may not believe in myself, I may get into an accident, I may have low self-esteem, I may get discouraged or depressed, I may get a speeding ticket, I may lose a lot of money, or I may not think I can achieve a career goal in my life. I deal with the same challenges in my life as anyone else. The difference between others and myself is how I *respond* to the challenges or adversities. It's not *what happens to me* in my life, it's *how I take it*!

In 1993, a reporter once asked Rose Kennedy, "There have been four tragic deaths in your family. How can you be so cheerful?" She replied, "The Lord would not give me a burden I could not handle. If a bird sings after a storm, why shouldn't I?"

Any time I think a problem is *out there*, the thought is really the problem. If I feel that people are mad at me, my initial perception is that *I* have a problem. However, the reality is that *they* have a problem. Do you recall the classic story about a man searching for a lost article on the street, under the light of a street lamp? When asked where he lost it, the man replied "Over there." He was then asked, "But why are you looking here?" And the man replied, "Because there's more light here."

I don't want to be looking for solutions in the wrong place. That idea is worth saying again, in different words: *I'm not going to find what I'm looking for unless it is where I'm looking.* If I take stressful events personally, I am looking in the wrong place. I must learn not to take stressful events personally. I must learn to react creatively to events by activating my success mechanism (through positive simulations and positive self-talk). It may be awkward at first, but I need to learn the habit of *instinctively* reacting to situations in a manner that will provide me with the greatest possible benefit.

Do I want to be a more effective leader? Yes! Do I want to experience less stress, worry, and anxiety about the future? Yes! Do I want to respond productively to negative situations in my life? Yes! Do I want to be fast, flexible and focused in achieving my personal goals? Yes! Do I want to live a happy, more rewarding life? Yes! Do I want to increase my performance effortlessly? Yes! Am I ready to develop the self-management qualities of all high achievers and highly effective leaders? Yes! Will I do everything in my power to cultivate the habit of maintaining a positive attitude? Yes! And if someone should ask me why I'm so enthusiastic about my job or my life, I will tell them I'm on a new drug called *endorphins.*

I said at the beginning of this chapter that I had not yet made an iron-clad commitment. Now I see that there is solid biological evidence to support the positive simulations and self-talk process. In fact, there is so much evidence from so many different sources that any residual resistance I have had to this process is essentially gone. Now it is just a matter of doing it.

Action Steps for this chapter:

A note about action steps and self-development in general. One of the great ironies of self-development practices is that when we attempt to do them and fall short, all we may accomplish is to add another layer of concern to our already stressful lives. By this time you will hopefully have begun doing the action steps previously suggested. Will you be doing all of them, all the time? Probably not. It takes a while to build new habits. Don't be discouraged if you find yourself sometimes slipping, forgetting, doubtful, or just too plain worn out to do them. Every little bit helps. So a word to the wise. Take it easy. Relax. Enjoy. Have fun. Laugh. Do what you can do. Give yourself a little credit for what you *are* doing and don't worry about what you're not doing. Doing self-development exercises regularly doesn't come from forcing yourself to be disciplined, it comes from the pleasure of knowing you are doing the right thing, that this is something that is really good for you. And this, in turn, leads to the development of the new habits of doing them easily and naturally.

And on this basis, if you promise you won't get stressed out, here's a reminder of the things you can (not should) be doing.

1) Have you been doing the restful alertness exercise to open all the pathways to your subconscious robot? You know, the one about listening for the bird's call.

2) I know you have done some positive visual simulations, and have made some positive verbal statements about yourself (with lots of gusto?). Keep it up.

3) Have you taken the time to create composite physical pictures of you achieving your goals? If not, you may want to do this now.

4) Have you written down any success statements? If not, this is a good time. (Remember, first person, present tense.)

5) Have you begun to act, in some ways, as if you are already the person you want to be? It's a powerful exercise that will put you on the path to achieving your goals.

6) Have you been able to change anything in your morning and nighttime habits in order to begin and end the day more positively? Even small changes help. Give it a try.

7) Remember about "faking it"? If you haven't written anything down in preparation for a bad day, review Chapter 4 for details.

7

A Reminder Chapter

This book is for more than casual reading. It is my daily guide and reminder. I want to constantly remind myself that I am building a competency model of all highly effective leaders—and I have a lot to remember. One of the points I *do* remember is that we all tend to be forgetful; *out of sight, out of mind.* And being mentally proactive is a distinct change from my former behavior in which thoughts, feelings and pictures just floated into and out of my mind without my having any control over them. So I find it helpful to regularly and frequently review what I have learned. This list below doesn't cover all I have learned, but it is a good mind-jogger. Let's see how I do with it.

I AM CONTROLLED BY THE MENTAL PICTURES I FORM

I've got this one cold. My conscious judge causes my subconscious robot to record what I say, see, think and feel, and my robot tells me what I can and can't do.

$V \times I = R$, VIVIDNESS $\times$ IMAGINATION = REALITY

I'm okay with this one, too. The more clearly I imagine my successes, the more strongly they will be imprinted in my robot, and the more my robot will tell me that I CAN!

WINNERS SIMULATE WINNING

By now I've read so many stories about how high achievers imagine their accomplishments in advance that I am convinced it works.

DO WITHIN WHEN I AM WITHOUT

This is related to the above. This says to me, rehearse and practice in my imagination when the physical means are absent. This has already helped me a great deal in my profession

"GOOD MORNING, YOU ARE TERRIFIC!"

This also really works. When I prepare for sleep with positivity, I sleep better, and when I begin the morning with encouragement and affirmations, I perform better.

SSAFBD: SAY IT, SEE IT, ACT IT, FEEL IT, BECOME IT—AND DO IT!

I understood this intellectually from the beginning, but it took me a while longer to really absorb it. But when I did, WOW! When I say it, see it and act it, I can really *feel* it. And when I feel like a very successful person, I start to become that person. And as I start to become that very successful person, I see myself actually performing in that way. This is powerful stuff!

CONTINUOUS PERFORMANCE IMPROVEMENT —CPI3030

I remember the research on this. Regular, spaced intervals are the key. 30 minutes a day for formal practice and, increasingly, my waking hours are becoming more habituated to positive, high-achieving thoughts and speech.

WINNING AND EXCELLENCE ARE MOSTLY DUE TO PERSONAL AND PEOPLE SKILLS

I am not ignoring my technical competence, but I am now very, very aware of how I look, how I talk and how I treat others.

PERSONAL AND PEOPLE SKILLS DEPEND ON A POSITIVE ATTITUDE

This is tricky, because I don't want to fall into the trap of worrying about whether or not my attitude is positive. So I think about the laughing clubs in India and about the horse entering a bar and the bartender says "Why the long face?" Then I visualize all the good hormones starting to course into my brain. And something interesting happens. As I start to think about all the things that make up a productive attitude, my attitude does become more positive. Neat!

OPTIMISTS HAVE MORE BRAIN CAPACITY THAN PESSIMISTS

This is a positive feedback loop. As my attitude gets better, I know my brain power increases. The knowledge of this gives my attitude a boost. This attitude boost increases my brain power. And so on.

I WILL REMAIN OR BECOME WHAT I MOST BELIEVE ABOUT MYSELF

This is related to *SSAFBD* above and is another positive feedback loop. As I say it, see it, act it, feel it, become it and do it, each of these steps help me to believe that I *really am* a very successful high-achiever. And the more I really believe it, the more effectively I can do each of the steps.

WHEN I THINK, SPEAK AND ACT LIKE AN EFFECTIVE LEADER
I BECOME AN EFFECTIVE LEADER

I think this one speaks for itself.

Now I've confirmed that I understand the basic principles of everything I've learned to this point. I'm ready to go on.

8

SELF-ESTEEM AND SELF-CONFIDENCE IN PROFESSIONAL DEVELOPMENT

Some days I think that before I barge on ahead, maybe I should pause for a moment and make certain I really understand what I'm talking about when it comes to *self-esteem* and *self-confidence*. Other days when I am reading this chapter I want to skip the conceptual part and get right to the how-to tips on self-esteem and self-confidence, so I go directly to the section on Self-Transformational Techniques. (You can certainly do the same.)

Now even though this first part is conceptual I don't want to engage in psychological jargon here, I just want to keep it simple. So in plain words what, really, is self-esteem? Well, it's what I think of myself. Do I respect, like and accept myself? Do I believe I am a worthy person? Worthy of what? Of happiness...of deserving high achievement and the fruits of success? And if I am a worthy person, what is it that makes me worthy? I can give an answer in religious terms, in the sense that we all are worthy by virtue of being human, but I'm looking for more than that here.

So what makes me feel that I am a worthy person? For one thing, I think I am basically a *good* person. All right, but what makes a good person? I believe most of us would say it is how we relate to others; that is, the degree to which we are kind, considerate, honest and fair in our relations with others.

Now I certainly try to behave this way to the best of my ability, and I believe that the vast majority of people do likewise. But if I think of myself as a good person, does that guarantee that I'll have high self-esteem? Not necessarily, because there's another important element—competence. If I feel like I'm a dummy, if I believe I'm largely incompetent, it's unlikely I'll have high self-esteem even if I relate like an angel to everyone else.

Of course, most of us feel highly competent in some areas and less so in others. This brings up that other term we use so freely: self-confidence. And I ask myself, am I self-confident? And the answer is, it depends on the specific area of expertise. For example, am I confident of my ability to play professional football? No. Am I confident about composing a new opera? No. Am I confident about preparing the world's greatest lasagna? Well...that's probably a gray area. But am I confident about giving one of the world's best corporate presentations? You bet I am! Am I confident about helping to enrich the lives of large numbers of people? Absolutely!

Now here's the key to this. My goals are not to play professional football, compose an opera or even make the world's greatest lasagna. My goals are, among others, to give terrific, inspiring presentations to inspire and enrich the lives of others. So one way for me to have high self-esteem is for me to have high self-confidence in *the areas that are important to me*. This is an important point, so I'll highlight it in large type to make sure it catches my attention.

SELF-ESTEEM IS CREATED BY SELF-CONFIDENCE IN AREAS THAT ARE IMPORTANT TO ME

Now some psychologists tell us that our self-esteem is largely built up from childhood experiences...with our parents, our siblings and friends, and our experiences at school, and that it is fixed by the time we are young adults. But is it really permanently fixed? From my own experience and that of thousands of others who have taken my seminars and used my audio and video materials, my answer is *absolutely not!* If my self-esteem was fixed after childhood, none of the self-development methods I employ would work, and few or none of my achievements in life would have happened. But the methods do work! My subconscious robot is quite capable of absorbing and recording all of the positive things I do, and telling my conscious judge that I am getting better and better; in other words, upgrading my self-confidence.

Now I have sorted out a fair amount here. For one, I know that my self-esteem is not fixed, that it can be enhanced by the techniques I use. And, as I said above, one way for me to have high self-esteem is for me to have high self-confidence in the areas that are important to me. So if I know what areas are important to me I can focus my attention and my techniques on them. And as I have shown in the previous chapters, positive simulations, self-talk and the other methods will help me improve in those areas. When my performance improves, my self-confidence is increased; and when my self-confidence in my abilities increases, up goes my self-esteem.

It's another positive feedback loop; better performance means greater self-confidence, which causes higher self-esteem, which enables even better performance, and so on. Jack Welch, former CEO of General Electric, was right on target when he said, "Empowering people with the self-confidence is the most important thing I do!"

But before I learn what I *can* do, I should mention what I've learned *not* to do. I have learned neither to *seek* nor *need* the approval of others for my actions, yet I am grateful when their approval is sincere. And I have learned to use the disapproval of others to look objectively at my own actions to see if the disapproval is warranted. I acknowledge my mistakes, correct them, and move on.

But I am determined that the disapproval of others, warranted or not, will not affect my self-esteem nor destroy my self-confidence. That is up to me alone.

Accountability to myself is important. I need to know when I have done poorly, but it is crucial that my self-criticism is constructive and encouraging. My actions are often less than perfect, yet I don't condemn myself (or others) for failures. Rather, my imperfections are a part of my uniqueness and value as a human being. I need to think of temporary failure as a challenge to be overcome.

Now almost everything I've said so far in this chapter has to do with *what* and *why*, which lays the foundation for understanding self-esteem and self-confidence. Still, we live in a world where we are almost constantly interacting with others, so *how* I relate to other people will play a large role in meeting my goals. The next section of this chapter is a collection of how-to's, and I am ready to learn practical, rapid and effective tips for enhancing and maintaining my self-esteem and self-confidence.

Self-Transformational Techniques
These are the techniques I use daily to optimize my self-esteem/self-confidence. Every waking moment I feed my subconscious self-images with positive thoughts about myself and/or my performances, so vividly and regularly that my recorded images are in time modified to conform to the new, higher standards. My body believes everything that I say; negative or positive self-talk is recorded by my self-image (my imagination) as facts to be stored as reality, and my body chemistry is altered accordingly. When I speak positively it gives me more energy to tackle the day. I possess positive winning feelings, and my personal motivation is increased to enhance my effectiveness level.

Perhaps the most important key to the continuous maintenance of high levels of my self-confidence are the practices of *positive self-talk* and *positive verbal interactions,* and the majority of these tips focus on these. For example, I am careful not to make such statements as, "I just don't have the patience or energy for that," "I'm really out of shape," "I never win anything," or, "It's going to be another one of those days!"

I am a winner and want to continue being a winner, so I use constructive self-talk every day. These are some frequent phrases:

+ I can
+ I look forward to
+ I'm worthy of respect and trust
+ I perform well under pressure
+ I believe in myself
+ I'll get the job done correctly
+ I am extremely competent
+ I accept the challenge
+ I'll find a way to do it
+ I am receptive to learning and growing
+ I am fast, focused and flexible

By using expressions like these I pay value to myself as an individual.

An indicator of someone's opinion of themselves is the way they accept a compliment. It is incredible how low-achievers belittle and demean themselves, even when others try to pay them value. How often have you, or someone you know, responded like this:

"I'd like to congratulate you on handling that situation with your client." "Oh, it was nothing, I was just lucky, I guess."

"Wow, that was a great shot you made!" "Yeah! I must have had my eyes closed."

"That's a good looking suit. Is it new?" "No, just some old thing I picked up."

The loser believes that the quality of humility should be pushed over the cliff into humorous humiliation. And the devastating fact is that the subconscious robot is always listening and accepts these negative barbs as facts to store as reality.

As a winner, I accept compliments by simply saying, "Thank you."

Jockey Steve Cauthen, after winning the Triple Crown, doesn't say "Gee, I almost fell off my horse." He says "Thank you." After completion of a successful mission, Neil Armstrong doesn't say "Oh, anyone could have done it," he says "Thank you" to the accolades from mission control. Michael Jordan says "Thank you." Tiger Woods says "Thank you" after a performance well done.

A part of my self-esteem is the quality of simply saying "Thank you" when I am complimented. This does two things. It tells my subconscious that I accept and deserve the compliment, and it avoids belittling the giver of the compliment. After all, if I pay you a sincere compliment and you respond by downplaying it or feigning indifference, that tells me, indirectly, that you don't trust my judgment.

A sincere "thank you," is also a way of expressing gratitude. *I try to be grateful daily*. Each week I write down who and what I'm thankful for. I didn't realize how thankful I was for my health until I hurt my back with my horses in April of 1986. I was running on the ground next to a filly and she pushed me. I felt good enough then, but the next day I couldn't walk. I now have sciatica. I learned how to control the pain and live with it, but now I really do appreciate my health. Do you?

And although there are sometimes exceptions, essentially everyone I meet and deal with is cooperating in some way to make my life more comfortable and convenient. For example, my car is almost always dependable. If I stop to think about it, it's fantastic! Fire and explosions constantly going on underneath the hood, quietly and safely, mile after mile. My car consists of tens of thousands of parts, all working together, all manufactured and assembled by thousands of people, all of whom are basically trying their best to build a good car. I may occasionally gripe about the cost of gasoline, but it is always available, having gone through hundreds of processes and untold numbers of people, to get from underground crude to the refined product.

Each day my mail arrives, the food I eat is safe, the telephone works, I have indoor plumbing to use, I have the pleasure of listening to music on my Bose sound system. I wear clothing made from cloth fibers invented by ingenious people with ingenious machines, sewed and formed by skilled workers.

And I'm thankful for so many other things: love at first sight, best friends, heroes, second chances, family traditions, the power of dreams, the gift of forgiveness, a sense of humor, unexpected rainbows, learning something new, easy-to-follow instruction manuals, outdoor weddings, privacy, loyalty, integrity, faith, good advice, a first kiss, the wisdom of old age...a hand to hold.

Feeling grateful for all of this...for life...not only makes me feel better, my gratefulness is a reflection of feeling deserving and worthy, and thus it enhances my self-esteem and self-confidence.

When I attend meetings, lectures and conferences, *I sit up front in the most prominent rows.* My purpose for going is to listen, learn, and possibly exchange questions and answers with the keynote speaker. If I hide in the rear, I am subconsciously telling myself that I don't deserve to be noticed.

I volunteer my own name first in every telephone call and whenever I meet someone new. This does two things. It invites a similar response and, by paying value to my own name in communication, I am developing the habit of paying value to myself as an individual.

I give a firm handshake when I meet someone. I don't squeeze someone's hand to cause pain or to impress them with my strength. Rather, I am sending a subconscious message to both myself and the recipient that I am serious about our relationship and what we might be able to accomplish together. That handshake tells a lot about me.

I maintain eye contact when speaking to someone. If I want to project an image of sincerity, involvement and success, downcast eyes or looking away will send exactly the wrong message. If for some reason I have difficulty looking directly in someone's eyes, then I will alternately look at the bridge of their nose.

I do something for others with a pleasant attitude and no strings attached—I don't seek praise or a favor in return. And if a return favor comes, so much the better.

I send cards or notes for special things. For example, I'll send a thank-you card to someone who was responsible for introducing me to a person I wanted to meet, or any time someone goes out of their way to help me.

I do something for myself. I may buy myself dinner, a book, or some other gift. This helps confirm that I believe I am deserving.

If I am about to tackle a job or goal that I feel is very difficult, when I may have self-doubt or get discouraged, this is what I do. *I write a list of my accomplishments and the positive qualities I'm proud of.* I concentrate on my successes, and this builds confidence in me that I can do it. People get discouraged because they recall past failures, so I need to focus on my strengths rather than my weaknesses.

What I focus on starts to dominate. I frequently remind myself to focus on what is important. I know that I will be given more of whatever I focus on, and I make sure my focus is positive.

I have a success wall in my home: posters about goals, courage, passion, teamwork, achievement and opportunity.

I carry an index card with me and write my goals on it. Throughout the day I may read it two to ten times depending on the need.

I have a motivational board in my office. On it I write names of exceptionally supportive and positive clients, names of companies I will be presenting to, pictures of goals I want to achieve in the next 30 to 60 days, and a list of happy, satisfied clients.

I also have a victory wall in my study. It holds plaques from companies that have said "thank you"—McDonald's, Coca-Cola, Automatic Data Processing and AT&T—as well as my diplomas and certificates.

And for the long term, I have a goals poster, showing those achievements planned for the next twenty years.

I also have a bust of Superman, to remind me that I am a *super human being.*

Most important I have photos of family members from childhood, to remind me where I came from.

Remember being tested on your reaction to the series of jokes in a previous chapter? How critical were you of them? How critical are you of everything around you? I read this book daily. If I want to develop more self-confidence, I will *concentrate on remembering what I like and ignore what I dislike.* If I focus on what I dislike, as low self-esteem people do, then I neglect everything that can benefit me. Instead, I will focus on what I like and on what benefits me, as high self-esteem people do.

I need to make changes in my internal responses rather than searching for changes in my external environment! I take pride and enjoyment in my current position. For 99% of the goals I want to achieve, I can achieve them in the corporation I'm working for now. How many times have I seen people move on to another job because of a few extra bucks or because they think the grass is greener? They're wrong! It looks greener because they observe it from a distance. If I look closely, I can see just as much doo-doo over there as over here. Many times people return to where they started after experimenting with other options. *I must realize that my current job is a vehicle to aid me in reaching my corporate and personal goals.* I may say, "This job is not what I thought it was." The truth is, "It's what I thought it was, *I'm not what I thought I was.*"

This is such an important point that I want to highlight it right here.

I NEED TO MAKE CHANGES IN MY INTERNAL RESPONSES RATHER THAN SEARCHING FOR CHANGES IN MY EXTERNAL ENVIRONMENT!

I need to set my own high internal standards. I am a unique human being, with unique skills, needs, desires and goals. So it really doesn't make sense to compare myself to others in terms of performance and achievements. That is like comparing what different people will eat for lunch, not knowing how much they've already eaten, what they like and dislike, dietary restrictions, and so on. So rather than comparing myself to others, I will compare my present performance with my past performances. Since I now know more, have acquired more skill, have established more connections, can I improve on my own past performance? You bet! Then I keep upgrading my own standards, lifestyle, behavior, professional accomplishments, and relationships. I continually raise my ideal self-image when it comes to my attitudes, goals, and interests.

My own self-esteem is related to the esteem I hold for Nature. I frequently take rides to observe nature—especially the sea and mountains. They have therapeutic value. Look at the word "esteem." Literally it means to appreciate the value of. Why do we stand in awe of the power and immensity of the sea, the uniqueness of a solar eclipse, the beauty of a mountain range, the size of a giant redwood, or the tranquillity of a sunset—yet at the same time downgrade ourselves? Didn't the same Creator make us? Are we not the most marvelous creation of all, able to think, experience, change our environment and love? I won't downgrade the product—myself— just because I haven't used it properly and effectively.

When doctors use an electroencephalograph (EEG) to record the electrical activity in a person's brain, they know that random brain waves indicate stress. However, when a person is experiencing the sight of the sea, a mountain range—and yes, even a golf course—brain waves are aligned to create "Brain Wave Coherence." In this relaxed meditative state, an ideal performance state is created. They are in "The Zone." I take time personally to visit the ocean and mountains several times throughout the year.

I maintain high self-esteem body language. I walk erectly and authoritatively in public and private, with a relaxed but determined pace. Individuals who walk erectly and briskly are usually confident about themselves and where they are going. I lean forward and nod as I'm speaking to someone. My arms and legs are uncrossed when I'm having a one-on-one conversation. I have pressed, clean clothes. My hair is neat and clean. I project on the outside how I feel about myself on the inside. Oh yes! I always carry breath mints. There is nothing worse than being with someone and instead of listening to what I'm saying they're thinking that my breath is bad. I want to make friends and influence people so I am aware of my breath and body odor. My personal grooming and lifestyle habits provide instantaneous projection on the surface of how I feel inside about myself.

I Smile! A smile is the most obvious external appearance of high self-esteem. A smile is the light in my window that says I'm a caring, sharing person. And it's the universal code that says I'm okay and you're okay, too.

Michael Eisner, CEO of Walt Disney, Inc., was interviewed on C-SPAN when he received the "Executive of the Year Trophy" at the Chicago Executive Club. He was asked why he had such dynamic and positive employees. His response was, "We interview fifty people at a time. We select the one that has the perpetual smile, eyes that light up with excitement, high energy and enthusiasm while going through the group interview."

I've said previously that our behavior and feelings interact. When I'm happy I smile, but also when I smile I become happy. The mind/body effect is a two-way system. In 1983, the University of California determined that the facial muscles are connected to the limbic gland in the brain. This gland triggers positive chemicals—

endorphins—that promote positive thoughts. A smile always triggers positive feelings in my body, the same way laughter does for all those 1000 Laughing Clubs in India.

After I get up in the morning, within five seconds I walk into the bathroom, look in the mirror, and smile. I engage in this Performance Ritual for 15 to 20 seconds. I do this for two reasons. First, it secretes positive enzymes. Second, it exercises my smile muscles so I'm able to smile more easily throughout the day or on the phone. (Incidentally, your voice sounds different when you smile as you're talking; people on the other end can "hear" you smiling.)

One of the most powerful activities to engage in daily to develop more self-confidence/self-esteem is *prayer*. I fall asleep praying at night. I also have developed the habit of praying for people throughout the day, if I believe they are less fortunate. This could be someone who is emotionally upset for one reason or another, someone who is sick or has been in an accident.

I'm sure there have been times when you have driven on a highway and experienced backed up traffic because of an accident. After 20-30 minutes you may pass the accident scene, and you find that the cars have been moved off the highway and onto the shoulder lane. The roadway is clear beyond the accident. Why is there backup traffic still? The reason is everyone is slowing down to see the accident. What possible good can that do? I've asked people why they do it, and they say they want to see if anyone got hurt. But, of course, that isn't the only reason. We want to see how crumpled each car is, we are fascinated by the drama of possible injury or death, and we are subconsciously relating the accident to ourselves, to the chances of our own involvement in an accident.

Instead of engaging in this behavior, here's what I do when there is an accident on the side of road. I focus on the license plate of the car in front of me and select one number from it. If the license plate reads "465-978," for example, I may select the number 6 and say that many Hail Marys for the accident victims.

What has all of this to do with self-esteem and self-confidence? When I engage in this kind of behavior, I feel that in some small measure I am helping the world and the people in it, that I am contributing something to the overall goodness of Creation. And I am a part of that goodness that has been bestowed upon me.

Another thing I can do to develop and affirm a high self-confidence level is to *establish and maintain a daily personal plan of action in developing my potential.* This is an investment in my own knowledge and skill development. The only real security is the kind that's inside me. I listen to tapes, CDs, CD-ROMs, and attend seminars on personal and professional development. The best time for me to listen is while I'm driving. My car is my University of Super Achievers. I take charge!

Up until now I've shared a few ideas that I follow daily to optimize my confidence level. But I need also to understand that many things happen in my environment to lower my self-esteem.

Many people engage in self-sabotage daily by creating anti-motivational blocks for themselves. Unlike them, I mustn't engage in compulsive, negative, self-defeating speech patterns that will imprint on my subconscious robot and reduce my potential. With this truth in mind, *it is essential that I learn to control my language.* This is important enough for me to repeat it right here.

IT IS ESSENTIAL THAT I LEARN TO CONTROL MY LANGUAGE

I must rethink key words that herald self-sabotage so I can change a negative to a positive.

In the past when I heard the word "no" it meant rejection. Instead, I need to interpret it instead to mean, *"not at this time."*

The word "can't" is usually associated with a lack of belief. Instead my interpretation should be *"possibly unable to do this at this time; what can I do to make it more possible, and if not possible what can I do as an alternative?"*

The word "but" is like erasing what I said previously. For example, "I want to increase sales *but* deliveries are backed up." Instead, I can make the meaning more positive by saying "I want to increase sales, *even though* deliveries are *not yet up to speed."*

"Too bad," "If only," "I should have," "I wish," and "I'll try" all indicate that I am a bad decision maker and are recorded by my robot as failure. Instead I say, "Next time I'll do it!"

"Take it easy," can sound too passive. Instead say, "Go for it!" "Take control!" "Have a great day!"

If I should hear anyone use negative or overly-passive words in a business setting, I say to myself, "Cancel! Cancel!" so they don't affect me negatively. Even if it's my boss, I say, "Cancel! Cancel!" to myself.

Another place to control my language is when someone asks me, "How are you?" If my answer is, "Not too bad," that's a 68/100 in my book. "Pretty good," is only a 71. So when someone asks me how I am, I always respond with the words that secrete endorphins in my brain: "Great," "Fantastic," "Excellent," "Terrrrrific!"

I replace the word "problems" with "challenges" because winners see problems as opportunities to challenge ability and determination.

I replace "failure" with "temporary inconvenience" or an "opportunity to develop internal strength" or a "learning experience."

I eliminate the words "won't," "don't," and "not" from my vocabulary. What images does the subconscious record when I say "don't," "won't," or "not"? None, I have no images. The subconscious robot doesn't understand negated words. "I won't be late," means to the subconscious, "be late." "I don't want you to go in the street," means "go in the street." "Don't touch that knickknack," means, "touch it."

So how do I motivate someone by the reverse of an idea? I phrase it positively. For example, instead of saying "I don't want your part of the presentation to be slow-moving," I'll say "I'd like your part of the presentation to be crisp and quick-moving." Or instead of saying "Please be careful not to mess up again on the cost figures," I'll say "It's really important that your cost figures be completely accurate."

When I'm speaking to myself I do the same thing. Instead of "I won't go broke" I say "I will maintain financial stability." Instead of "I won't be late" I say "I'll get to my appointments early." Instead of, "I won't procrastinate" I say "I take action immediately when something needs to be done."

I say what I want instead of what I don't want. Let me repeat that.

I SAY WHAT I WANT INSTEAD OF WHAT I DON'T WANT

Nevertheless, negated speech patterns are so prevalent and such longstanding habits that it takes some thought and focus to alter them. Here are a few more negative examples.

"Don't worry!" "Don't forget!" "I won't forget." "No problem." "Don't stop." "Don't do that!" "Not like that!" "Oh, it's nothing." "Not a chance." "Don't start that again." "I can't help it." "I can't stand it." And so on.

How many times have we all heard and said these statements? It's a real challenge to eliminate these phrases because we have all developed habit patterns utilizing them for years and years. Yet it can be done. Instead of "I won't forget," try "I'll remember."

Instead of responding with "No problem," try "I'll do it" or "My pleasure."

Instead of " Not like that!" try "Do it like this."

But some phrases are harder to find substitutions for. For example, how do you replace "Don't start that again!"? Well, depending on the situation you might say, "I'd like us to talk candidly about this subject in a calm manner."

I realize it takes discipline to develop new habit patterns in speaking. It takes awareness, focus, persistence and patience—just like it does to become proactive in our thinking, our visual simulations and how we act. Once again I remind myself that I am building a competency model of all high-achievers. And, once again, I ask myself, am I *really* determined to use every tool I can to enhance my self-esteem and self-confidence; to employ those tools I have learned to become the very best person I can be; and to use every technique I know in order to attain my goals?

Whether I am working alone or with large numbers of others, I understand that I am the CEO of myself, or as the poet put it, "I am the captain of my soul." I take this CEO responsibility seriously. It means that I am responsible for creating the very best person I can be. The above tips have given me a powerful boost in this direction, and I believe they will do the same for you.

Action Steps:

We're looking at a number of behavior changes in this chapter. Because of this I think it's worthwhile here to repeat a part of the Action Steps notes from a previous chapter.

Don't be discouraged if you find yourself sometimes slipping, forgetting, doubtful, or just too plain worn out to do these exercises. Every little bit helps. So a word to the wise. Take it easy. Relax. Enjoy. Have fun. Laugh. Do what you can do. Give yourself a little credit for what you are doing and don't worry about what you're not doing. Doing self-development exercises regularly doesn't come from forcing yourself to be disciplined, it comes from the pleasure of knowing you are doing the right thing, that this is something that is really good for you. And this, in turn, leads to doing the new habits easily and naturally.

Action Steps for this chapter:

1) Write down 6-10 areas of importance to you. If you can do it, prioritize them. Try to focus each day on the highest priorities.

2) Try to become more aware of your own speech patterns when you interact with others. Be on the lookout for negated statements you make.

3) Try to be aware of how you respond when someone compliments you.

4) When you answer the telephone, try starting with a pleasant "hello," followed by giving your name.

5) Try to look objectively at your job or your business situation and see what potential you can discern, both for yourself and for others who are involved.

6) Re-read the tips given in this chapter and choose several for practice that feel most comfortable to you.

9

THE ABC OF POSITIVE SELF-DETERMINATION

Up to this point I have learned a lot. For example, I understand how my body produces helpful or unhelpful chemicals based on my conscious thoughts and feelings, and how these thoughts and feelings are influenced by my levels of self-esteem and self-confidence. I have learned the importance of positive self-talk and the effectiveness of spaced repetitions. I know how to get rid of old, negative habits and learn new ones and I have read the many tips that take advantage of all this knowledge.

I have learned all of this. But will my actions actually reflect all that I have learned? This depends on many factors, but most of all on my thoughts (the only things in life that I have absolute control over) which will largely determine my actions.

All of this generally falls under the category of self-control, or self-determination. (Because the phrase *self-control* has a connotation of denying ourselves enjoyable things, I prefer *self-determination,* which has a broader feeling.) After all, life is a do-it-to-myself program and I know that if I exert control over what happens to me, this will allow me to be happier and to be able to choose more appropriate responses to whatever occurs. Voltaire likened life to a game of cards: "Each player must accept the cards life deals him or her. But once they are in hand, he or she alone must decide how to play the cards in order to win the game." Writer John Erskine put it a little differently: "Though we sometimes speak of a primrose path, we all know that a bad life is just as difficult, just as full of work, obstacles, and hardships, as a good one. The only choice is the kind of life one would care to spend one's efforts on."

In controlling my thoughts and, by this, practicing self-determination, I have found that three areas are of vital importance: the ABC of *accountability, blame* and *choice*. I'm going to begin this discussion with *blame*.

Blame

At an old synagogue in Eastern Europe there was a conflict over tradition. When certain prayers were said, half of the members stood up and the other half remained seated. The half that stood up shouted at the others to stand up also, and the half that remained seated shouted equally for their brethren to sit down. Both the standers and the sitters were convinced they were right and they each blamed the other group for flouting tradition.

They consulted the rabbi but he didn't know which group was keeping the tradition correctly and which wasn't. So the rabbi decided to seek the advice of an old man who was one of the original founders of the synagogue. In the midst of the shouting, the rabbi, together with the leader of the standers and the leader of the sitters, approached the old man. Raising his voice to be heard above the din, the rabbi described the conflict and the leader of the sitters blurted out "The conflict is the fault of the standers! Is it not the tradition to remain seated during this prayer?"

"No," said the old man, "that is not the tradition."

Then the leader of the standers gleefully shouted, "Aha, then the sitters are at fault! Is it not the tradition to stand during this prayer?"

"No," said the old man, "that is not the tradition."

Then the rabbi interrupted and said, "But the congregants are constantly yelling, blaming each other for sitting or standing!"

The old man paused for a moment, then replied "Of course. *That* is the tradition."

As we all know, it is easy to avoid being completely truthful with ourselves. It's easy to blame something other than ourselves for our condition, and to believe that circumstances or other people have forced us to do what we do, and thus we are not free to choose our own actions. This has several results. First, we are able to absolve ourselves of responsibility for our condition—but look, if I say my condition isn't my fault, then what happens to my control? I have effectively given it up to someone else! And if I give it to someone else, what does that do to my ability to improve my situation?

So if I blame others for my misfortune, I'm actually giving them control over my life. Blaming others keeps me from taking responsibility for myself. It is a surrender of my power. Wow! That's an important insight for me to remember; so I'm going to repeat it right here.

WHEN I BLAME OTHERS FOR MY MISFORTUNE, I'M ACTUALLY GIVING THEM CONTROL OVER MY LIFE.

And further, when I allow myself to succumb to the disease of *blame-itis,* I not only lose my control over my own life, I find it is related to the diseases of *victim-itis* and *excuse-itis.* If I allow myself to be a victim, someone pummeled by negative outside influences, doesn't that have a bad effect on my self-confidence? And what about *excuse-itis?* This is the syndrome where I come up with excuses for not achieving what I want in life. How does excuse-itis affect my view of reality? Don't excuse-itis and victim-itis cloud my view of reality and prevent me from seeing actual alternative possibilities?

Speaking of excuses, I find it sad that so many people blame their parents for the reason they are not achieving what they want or are not as successful or happy as they would like to be. Have you ever heard a teenager say something like, "Poor me, I'm only flipping hamburgers at McDonald's"? In response to statements like this, Bill Gates said "Flipping hamburgers is not beneath your dignity. Your grandparents had a different word for burger flipping; they called it opportunity." Gates went on to say, "If you mess up, it's not your parents' fault, so don't whine about your mistakes, learn from them."

Accountability

In Pennsylvania, a burglar entered the house of a vacationing family. When he had filled his sack with valuables he decided to leave the house by way of the garage. But he discovered that the garage door opener was not working and he couldn't raise the garage door. Then he realized he couldn't re-enter the house because the connecting door to the house had locked when he had shut it. The house was somewhat isolated, and no one could hear the burglar's shouts for help. The family remained away for another eight days, and the burglar subsisted on a case of soda and a large bag of dry dog food. After the family returned, the burglar managed to avoid being convicted and, a short time later, sued the family, claiming his enforced stay had caused him extreme mental anguish. The jury agreed and upheld his claim for $500,000!

Well, I can't undo all the cases of non-accountability I read about, but I *can* try to be personally accountable. That is, I can assume responsibility for my actions and my condition, and admit—to myself and to others when appropriate—my own mistakes and failures. It is important that I do this without taking it personally. If I have done something badly, I can recognize my *specific* mistake and plan how to do it better next time, at the same time acknowledging that I am still a competent, decent person.

On the flip side, I know that undue modesty has a negative effect on myself and on others (when received compliments are belittled, etc.), and that it is okay—no, it's more than okay, it's necessary—to take pride in my real accomplishments.

I RESOLVE TO TAKE BOTH CREDIT AND BLAME FOR MY SUCCESSES AND FAILURES IN LIFE

Choice

Bill received a parrot for his birthday. This parrot was fully grown, with a bad attitude and a worse vocabulary. Every other word was an expletive. Those that weren't expletives were, to say the least, rude. Bill tried hard to change the bird's attitude and was constantly saying polite words, stroking the bird, playing soft music, anything he could think of to try and set a good example.

Nothing worked. He yelled at the parrot. He shook it and the bird got more angry and more rude. Finally, in a moment of desperation, Bill put the parrot in the freezer. For a few moments he heard the bird squawking, kicking, and screaming—then suddenly there was total quiet.

Frightened that the parrot might be dying, he quickly opened the freezer door. The parrot calmly stepped out onto Bill's extended arm and said "I'm sorry that I might have offended you with my bad language and actions. I ask your forgiveness. I will endeavor to correct my behavior."

Bill was astonished at the bird's change in attitude and was about to ask what had made such a dramatic change when the parrot continued, "May I ask what the chicken did?"

Now the parrot in this story had little choice. Although vulgar, the parrot was smart and quickly realized that a change in behavior was necessary. Occasionally we are placed in similar situations; that is, situations where we have little choice but to quickly decide in a certain way, such as jumping out of the way of an oncoming vehicle. But more often the consequences are not quite so immediate. For example, is it true when I think to myself, "I have to eat"? No! I can starve if I choose! In spite of what my body is telling me, I make the final decision. I eat because I *decide* to, and I decide to because if I don't I will be uncomfortable and my body will suffer the consequences.

And again a bit more subtle. Is it true when I think "I have to get up," or "I have to go to work," or "I have to pay taxes"? Do I really have to pay taxes? No I don't! I can earn just a little and not owe any taxes; or earn a lot but spend a lot of time and energy learning how to invest in tax deferral programs; or try to beat the IRS; or give up my citizenship, or go to prison.

Still, all these kinds of decisions are fanciful. But what about getting a bit closer to reality? What if I am working with someone that I don't get along with very well. What are my options? Well, I can try more effective communication...maybe it's simply a misunderstanding. Or maybe I can try to be more empathetic and understand the other person's concerns better. Or maybe I can find an effective intermediary. If these don't work, perhaps I can find ways to minimize my interaction with this person but still do my job well. Failing that, I might be able to be transferred to a location or position away from this person. And failing that, I can quit. But if none of these solutions are feasible, *I can change my response to this person.*

We all have choices in our behavior, including several levels of choices. I can accept conditions as they are or I can decide to change them. If I'm unable to do this, I can remove myself from the environment. If I'm unable to, or choose not to do this, I can change my thoughts to adapt to the circumstances. Whatever I decide to do, it is important for me to understand that I choose my response to *all* circumstances, *all* the time. Let's repeat that as well as an important point from the previous chapter.

I CHOOSE MY RESPONSE TO ALL CIRCUMSTANCES, ALL THE TIME

I NEED TO MAKE CHANGES IN MY INTERNAL RESPONSES RATHER THAN SEARCHING FOR CHANGES IN MY EXTERNAL ENVIRONMENT

So each day I decide whether or not I will go to work, what I will do, how I will react to others, and hundreds of other mundane decisions every hour of every day. Any time I think "I have to" it builds internal resentment—I feel that I "have to" because if I don't do it I will be hurt in some way. But thinking and speaking this way places me in a psychological prison.

Instead of thinking "I have to," I must constantly remind myself that the one area I have control over is my response to circumstances. This constant reminder allows me to understand that I'm not a victim. And whenever I feel I'm being forced to do something, I must also remind myself that I am viewing the circumstance incorrectly, and something in my viewpoint needs to change.

I can actually feel the change in my mental attitude and in my body when I think or say, "I want to read this book," "I have decided to go to work early," "I choose to stay late at work," "I choose to attend this seminar," or "I have decided to study," or, "I've decided to go for what I truly want." And the feeling I have is good. By developing the habit of being aware that I have choices, I am empowering myself. I am in control of my life.

Now that I have formed the habit of being aware of my choices, I can approach the exciting challenge of what choices to make. And here I will pause for a moment to make another declaration that certainly stands among the most important. The essence of a highly effective person is the ability to subordinate an impulse to a value.

THE ESSENCE OF A HIGHLY EFFECTIVE PERSON IS THE ABILITY TO SUBORDINATE AN IMPULSE TO A VALUE.

What do we mean by values? All of us hold deeply-felt personal values. These vary across a wide range even though we may not be consciously aware of all of them. For example, most of us hold *physical values* about maintaining our bodies in good health, and perhaps the attributes of strength, vitality, agility, grace and attractiveness. We have *intellectual values* that may include discovering new things, being creative, using our minds to their fullest extent, the gradual acquisition of wisdom, etc. *Psychological values* might include character, personality, friendship, trustworthiness, integrity and caring. Among *financial values* we might hold are gaining of independence, freedom, power, luxury, philanthropy, influence, etc. And lastly, there are the *spiritual values,* governing the need to seek meaning and purpose in life, some kind of relationship with the Creator, and so on.

We call these deeply-held beliefs our *values*. The term, is not accidental, for our beliefs have real value—they are worth something. In fact, our values are the foundation for everything we believe in and for everything we accomplish in life. If I believe, for example, that it is important to have a healthy and energetic body, then one of my goals will be to make the choices that will help maintain myself in good physical condition.

Now as we all know from our own experiences, it isn't always easy to subordinate an impulse to a value (think food, sex, money, truthfulness and envy for starters). But one of the ways that strengthens my ability to hold to my values and make right decisions in the face of temptation or adversity is to be aware of them. And one of the ways of maintaining awareness of my values is by writing them down, and comparing them with my goals.

This has several benefits. One is that I occasionally need to look at my own life to see if my goals really reflect my values (if not, my goals must change if I really believe in my values). This, in turn, reminds me whether or not I am on track and making progress towards my goals. And in order to know if I am really making progress towards my goals, I am forced to pay attention to the process of how I will reach my goals. And lastly, I have to look at my daily activities to see if they are actually helping or hindering me from reaching my goals.

Short-, intermediate- and long-term goals are also significant. For example, one of your values might be to use your intellectual capacity to its fullest extent. From this value, a long-term goal might be for you to decide to go back to school to get an MBA. Your intermediate-term goal might be to complete courses that apply to an MBA program, and your short-term goal might be to do some independent learning in preparation. Then your daily activities might include doing a minimum amount of business reading each day.

Comparing and tracking values and goals provides a way of monitoring daily activities to make sure they are supporting your personal values. This procedure can sound simplistic, but it is an extremely powerful tool for keeping on the track to success.[1]

I said above that one of the characteristics of high achievers is their ability to let their values determine choices rather than their impulses. And the ability to subordinate an impulse to a value depends in large degree on having a clear and strong sense of your own values. The process of identifying your life values, making sure they complement your short- and long-term goals, and verifying that your daily activities will lead you to these goals is highly

---

[1]Although the words have been changed, the ideas presented here are from the book *For Love & Money* by Roy O. Williams.

beneficial. It is a means of bringing your principles and activities into productive balance.

Another characteristic of high-achievers is their ability to do long-term thinking and long-term planning. There is a story told by an American who lived in Japan for many years and worked in a small town in a rural area. Each day he walked to and from his workplace along a country road. Alongside the road was a rice paddy, and each day he noticed a farmer, standing upright and treading on a water wheel. The water wheel was connected to a series of wooden troughs that distributed the water throughout the field. The American noticed that the paddy was empty; nothing was planted there.

Each day he gave a friendly wave to the farmer, who returned it. Month after month this went on, and nothing was ever planted there. The seasons came and went, and years passed without change. Each day the farmer was there steadfastly pedaling on the water wheel.

Finally, twenty years passed. Both men were now old. The American still walked to work, and the Japanese farmer still pedaled the water wheel. One day the American paused to rest and, after doing so, walked over to the farmer and greeted him with *ohaio gozaimas* (good morning). The farmer returned his greeting, and the American said, "I have seen you here year after year for these past twenty years, and nothing has ever been planted. Will you please tell me why you are doing this?" And the farmer replied, "I'm preparing this field for my grandson."

The responsibilities of daily life are often so compelling and so time-consuming that we pursue only short-term interests. In addition, the structure of the American marketplace mandates a sharp focus on near-term results. The result of all of this is that long-term planning is often not given the attention it deserves and requires; long-term goals cannot be attained with short-term planning. So if I am to become as successful as I desire, I have to establish clear goals five, ten and even more years ahead.

This chapter is titled The ABC of Positive Self-Determination, and the premise is that if my actions are actually going to reflect all that I have learned up to this point, then it is up to my thoughts to guide me in the right direction—after all, my thoughts are the only things over which I have total control. So it's up to my thoughts.

The *A* of ABC is for accountability. I know that I have to be completely honest with myself about my mistakes as well as my successes. The main point to remember about accountability is to understand that If I have done something badly, I can recognize my *specific* mistake and plan how to do it better next time, at the same time acknowledging that I am still a competent, decent person.

The *B* of ABC is for blame. And blame-itis, I said, is related to victim-itis and excuse-itis. And the important point to remember here is that when I blame, when I am a victim, I give up control to someone or something else. And that limits my choices.

And the *C* of ABC is for choice. I think the two most important points to remember about this are these two powerful statements:

I need to make changes in my internal responses
rather than searching for changes in my
external environment.

and

The essence of a highly effective person
is the ability to subordinate an impulse to a value.

In 1999 I gave a sales presentation to Dan Sullivan, Senior Vice President of the Buckley, Thorne, Messina Company in Needham, Massachusetts (today they are Advantage Sales and Marketing/ESM). After all of the material in this book up to this point had been presented, I asked him if he could identify another essential quality of high achievers that I hadn't yet covered. He spoke and, as he did, I noticed an impressive ring on his finger. Dan had played in the 1969 and 1970 Superbowls with the Baltimore Colts, who won in 1970. He not only identified the next quality of high achievers, he had walked the talk.

Action Steps for this chapter:

1) On a large piece of paper or on your computer, prepare a table, listing your personal values (hint: use the five categories of intellectual, psychological, financial, physical and spiritual).

2) Add your important long-term goals, and see if your goals complement your values. If not, how will you need to change your goals to reflect your deeply-held values?

3) Add the intermediate- and short-term steps you will need to take in order to accomplish your long-term goals.

4) Look at your daily activities and ask yourself if they are really helping you to accomplish your goals. If not, how will you change them?

5) Resolve to let your personal values dictate your decisions—as much as you can, starting right now!

10

COURAGE—A SELF-MANAGEMENT SKILL

Once again, I begin a chapter of my CPI (continuous performance improvement) guidebook, by reminding myself that personal character traits are of vital importance for professional development, for becoming and remaining a high achiever. And I believe that some of my own, and others', experiences can help to shed light on how courage can be developed.

In 1996 I became the caregiver to my mother, an experience that provided many new, enjoyable experiences for both of us. One of the activities my mom and I participated in daily was playing poker. At first I intentionally let my 83-year-old mother win 8 out of 10 games. This not only enhanced her pleasure in playing, it was fun for me to watch her self-confidence skyrocket. As she gradually got better at it, I didn't have to "throw" so many games. Then one day she mentioned that a busload of senior citizens was going to the Foxwoods Casino and would I lend her $100 because she could make me a lot of money. Her expectations were a bit unrealistic, but the point I want to make is that through the successful experience of playing cards she developed the confidence and courage to take action that she'd never done before.

In my own case I, too, learned that courage is an important characteristic of success. And from reading about, talking to and personally knowing many high achievers, I confirmed that courage—a form of inner psychological strength—plays a large role in their lives as well. While we are all born with different gifts, no one is automatically courageous. So what makes a person courageous? I mean, it's all well and good to talk about courage, and it's great to *want* to be courageous...but how does someone actually *become* courageous? How is courage developed? Some of the words that are related to the development of courage are confidence, determination, persistence, faith, purpose and (one of my favorites) the iron will of a champion. These all support the development of courage in one way or another. Or here's another way of looking at it: what are the obstacles to courage?

I have found that a main obstacle is fear. Fear is a major deterrent to success, so I needed to learn how to develop an organized response in the presence of fear. I began by asking myself, where is fear? And I answered by saying it's in my mind, in my imagination. And since fear is based on the self-imposed limitations I have formed in my imagination, the battle *against* fear must also take place in my imagination.

Let's see how this works.

In 1977 I left my former position as a vice-president in the advertising industry to become a consultant and professional speaker. I was attempting to do something I had never achieved before, and the prospects seemed scary as I had no previous successes to give me the courage to take action. I wanted to speak at McDonald's Corporation (Hamburger University), AT&T, ADP, Coca-Cola, IBM, Gloria Stevens Figure Salons, Reebok, Savin, Dunkin' Donuts, Walt Disney...the list goes on.

There were several steps I needed to initiate in order to develop more courage. First, I needed to change my focus. I needed to become a visionary and utilize Anticipation Simulation. I preplayed the future and began to simulate the end result. Then I went out and took photos of the logos on each of these company buildings:

the McDonald's sign in Westwood, MA; the Coca-Cola Sign in Needham, MA; the ADP sign in Waltham, MA, and so on.

I designed my own goal poster and looked at these pictures daily. The pictures helped trigger the mental simulations of speaking to these corporations. I rehearsed them relentlessly and then I began to visualize my presentation, and then feel the simulated accolades from the audience. I simulated receiving hundreds of testimonials saying how much it benefited them. *I visually simulated the end result I wanted to achieve.*

ANTICIPATION SIMULATION IS A PRECURSOR OF COURAGE

The rest is history. Since that time I have presented my programs to several thousand McDonald's employees throughout the country. I was invited to Hamburger University on two occasions. The accolades were wonderful. The thousands of testimonials were outstanding. Yes, I have also presented to ADP, Coca-Cola, IBM, Gloria Stevens, and Savin. A current goal is to present to Reebok and Walt Disney.

The second step to develop more courage in my life was to *take action believing I will succeed* (rather than letting success surprise me). Taking action toward achieving a goal has the effect of reducing the fear of doing it. This is an important point; let me repeat it.

TAKING ACTION TOWARD ACHIEVING A GOAL REDUCES THE FEAR OF DOING IT

I take action to dissolve my fears. The action triggers positive feelings throughout my body, and the results are increased self-confidence and courage. Rudyard Kipling said, "Courage is not the absence of fear, it's moving forward in the presence of fear." And Mark Twain said, "Do the thing you fear and the death of fear is certain."

All high achievers possess the ability to overcome fear. My fear became an asset when I learned how to control it. Here is an example that prevented personal injury.

It was January of 1992, and it was snowing as I drove down Route 128 in Waltham, Massachusetts. It was already 5:00 p.m. and the roads were dark and slippery. Unexpectedly I began to skid to the right.

Ten years prior I would have slammed my brakes and landed in a snowy embankment, likely totaling my car for the third time. This would have been a reaction out of fear without thinking. The fear would have closed down the left side of my brain because of the cortisol secreted. I would have been left with only the right side, the emotional side.

But in those intervening years I learned a lot about driving on slippery roads. I learned that slamming on the brakes was the worst thing I could do in a skid, and that the best thing I could do in my front-wheel-drive car was to accelerate and allow the power of the engine to pull the car out of the skid. *And I learned to control my fear by forcing myself to think in crisis situations.*

So this time, in that brief moment when the skid occurred, I thought, and then floored the accelerator. That pulled me out of the skid, causing no harm to the surrounding cars or me. I responded by thinking and acting rationally in the presence of fear. In fact, after this event I became more confident driving in snow. Success breeds success.

This was a great learning experience, and from it I realized that one powerful way to develop more courage is to deliberately place myself in situations that cause me fear. I needed situations that took me outside my comfort zone so I would learn how to act calmly and swiftly. I realized that though fear is imaginary, it is a major deterrent to my development of courage and my ability to become a more prudent risk-taker. Fear is the major reason why I place limitations on myself.

Now, in my training programs, I get my students involved in *controlled* fearful activities, based on intensity of fear on a scale from 1 to 10.

Here is an example at Level 2. I ask twelve participants in my *Excellence in Leadership* seminar to assemble a puzzle. They do it in around 30-45 seconds. Then I ask them to beat the record of 2 and 1/2 minutes—blindfolded. At this point, apprehension, self-doubt, anxiety or fear may enter the equation. How do people react? How will they handle the situation when one of their senses is taken away?

My other training programs involve *Adventure Learning,* Outward-Bound-type experiences. Higher levels of fear are introduced to deliberately cloud participants' thinking and increase the stress levels; for example, rope climbs, 10, 20, 50 feet in the air, and white water rafting. Taken to its ultimate, there is the Level 10 of fear—an actual fire walk! Level 10 is the Trials by Fire Workshop where the students actually walk across a red-hot bed of coals at 1200 degrees without getting burnt.

Everyone knows that fire burns. But these students are learning how to deal with extreme adversity by changing their thoughts. It's easy to be skeptical until you have experienced this for yourself. But they learn that the *apparent* problem is not the *real* problem; it is our thought process that is the real problem. In other words, it's not what happens to me—it's how I take it!

I live in the Boston area and I enjoy following the Boston Marathons. Do you happen to remember the 1996 Boston Marathon? On her 22nd mile, Uta Pippig developed severe abdominal pains. She was going to quit but then she resolved to tough it out, and she went on to win the Marathon four miles later. As it turned out, she turned her adversity into an opportunity to learn and grow; her strength and confidence were greatly increased from the experience.

In fact, every adversity has the seed of an equivalent or greater benefit. Adversity builds character as long as we hold on to the lessons we learn. Five simple words, originally from an ancient Arabic saying, have allowed me to view adversity with some perspective. The words are *and this, too, shall pass.* This concept is so profound I want to repeat it here.

AND THIS, TOO, SHALL PASS

Have you heard this story about Tiger Woods? When he was twelve years old he missed a shot in a tournament and threw his club. Officials disqualified him for displaying unsportsmanlike conduct. A few weeks later, however, he returned and won the next tournament. One of his competitors, seeing how disappointed and upset he had been, asked him how he had been able to win. Tiger's comment was, "My Mom taught me how to turn a negative in my life into positive energy!" Tiger's Mom had said, "Focus on the next tournament. Let your clubs speak for you instead of getting upset or mad with the disqualification." Wouldn't it be wonderful if all parents taught their children to do this?

I like to use the phrase *turning a lemon into lemonade.* This is how I turn a negative into a positive. I first identify the negative in my life. I don't put it under the carpet and say it's not there. I'm not a cockeyed optimist. I tell myself to identify it but not to dwell on it. The more you think about it the bigger it gets.

Here are several examples, based on a series of true events that happened to me. They began in December of 1990. I was giving a presentation to Jim Edler, the Organizational Development Manager of General Electric in Lynn, MA. Before the presentation I got a sliver in my finger which hurt quite a bit. I managed to get through the presentation but on my way home on Route 128 I got a ticket. Then, when I arrived home, I found out that my computer had crashed. And then I sat on my glasses and broke them. The next day I was driving on the Mass Turnpike and my engine seized and died from an unsuspected oil leak. Three days later I received a letter from the motor vehicle registry. They informed me that I had lost my license for 30 days because that was my third ticket in one year. I had to return my license to them within 24 hours. I call these kinds of events the "Test of a Champion." This was my opportunity to see if I could practice what I preach. Would I utilize positive thinking, simulations and all the other procedures I had advocated so enthusiastically? How could I turn these lemons into lemonade?

This is what I thought and did. I managed to get the 2×4 out of my finger and was pleased that I had been able to perform well with pain. My computer blew out, so I hired a programmer and he taught me how to remedy it if it happened again. I broke my glasses, but that was okay because I needed new ones; the old ones were pitted and I'd been putting off replacing them. Then my car engine blew up; it was out of oil but the oil warning light had failed to come on. Yes, it was costly to have it repaired but I couldn't drive anyway because I had just lost my license.

Now the best part of it all is that I was able to fulfill one of my life fantasies. I had no license or car, so I hired a beautiful, white stretch limousine for 30 days. My chauffeur, an attractive and charming woman, was instructed to come to my door every morning with a rose. She transported me to my seminars and appointments with key clients. I took many of my clients out to lunch in the limo and really milked the experience for all it was worth. I not only enjoyed it myself, it helped boost my relationship with several clients.

Then when I finally got back my license, I was really grateful for it. I never realized what a privilege it was to drive my own car. But wait, there's more. The following day I went on an appointment in Boston. I was simulating getting a parking space outside an office building on High Street (in an area where parking spaces are very hard to find) and I did it. There was a parking spot right where I imagined it would be (anticipation simulation). Two hours later I came out and my car was gone! I went into the deli nearby and asked if they had seen anyone take it. "Yes," was the response, "the city towed it because you were illegally parked after 4:00 p.m." It was 5:00 p.m. at the time. I said, "Fantastic, I thought it was stolen." I called the impound lot and took a taxi to it. When the woman there said I owed $60, I said, "That's terrific. Thank you." Her response was, "You're the happiest person I've ever seen whose car we towed."

But my attitude was logical to me. When I have two negatives—either a car is stolen or it is towed—I choose to focus on the less painful of the two negatives. Then it becomes a positive. So my high school algebra teacher was correct when he taught me that two negatives do equal a positive. No matter what difficulty I deal with, I can always find the benefits of it *if I focus on looking for the benefits.* Let me repeat that.

FOCUS ON LOOKING FOR THE BENEFITS

A woman called me several years ago and informed me she was depressed, losing her job, and going through a divorce with three kids. She said, "I wish I was positive like you all the time." I said, "Pam, you and I have the same emotions. The difference between us is that you use your emotions as excuses to get depressed and stay down, a rationalization for why you shouldn't be a productive human being. You see, Pam, tough times make tough people. Tough times don't last, but tough people do!"

I learned this through many life experiences, and especially after reading Rabbi Kushner's book, *When Bad Things Happen to Good People.* In the book he says, "It's not *why* bad things happen to good people! Instead it's *when* bad things happen to good people." I felt he was speaking directly to me and saying, "Richard, there are two rules you must accept in order to play the game of life. The first is that life isn't fair, and the second is that pain doesn't last!"

Rabbi Kushner went on to tell how an experience that hurts also develops a potential for greater love inside us.

He suggests beginning to look for the benefits even while we are feeling emotional or physical pain, and that one of the benefits is greater sensitivity towards the pain, trials and needs of others.

Now my emotions act like the foghorn or light beacon for a ship entering a foggy harbor. They act as corrective feedback to put me on course and keep me on course. Most importantly they build an immunity within me toward future discouragement and distress.

I'm also inspired by other examples of great courage and perseverance. One I recall is the story of Burnell Wallace, who was a brilliant television news anchorwoman on Channel 5 in Bakersville, California. One day she was flying her Cessna 150 over the Rocky Mountains at 10,000 feet and the engine died. She desperately tried to find a landing location but there was none, and the plane crashed with a fiery explosion. Amazingly, she survived the crash and crawled her charred body out of the wreckage. Her hair and eyebrows were gone; her nose had melted; she was burned over 90% of her body. Yet she slowly crawled in agony for one mile, then two, then three, and finally four miles to a roadway. An 18-wheeler picked her up and transported her to a hospital that, miraculously, was only one mile down the road. The attendants ran out with a gurney, and rolled her into the emergency room. Two doctors were standing over her. One said, "She'll be dead in two hours." Burnell couldn't speak but screamed to herself, "I'm going to survive, don't give up on me." She tried to grab the white coat of one of the doctors, to give them hope. The other doctor said, "It's just a muscle spasm." She thought, "NO, NO, NO, I'll make it! I'm a fighter."

Well, she did make it. She wears a mask today, and is an example of extreme courage, persistence and tenacity in the face of terrible adversity. Rather than becoming depressed, Burnell now says, "You can if you think you can. It's not what happens to you, it's how you take it." Wow, what a woman!

There are so many other examples I could describe. How many times have I seen Rick Hoyt in the Boston Marathon? He was born with cerebral palsy, and doctors advised his parents to "put him away." But they didn't. At age 37, Rick is a graduate of Boston University and is working at Boston College, helping to design a new computer called Eagle Eyes that is controlled by eye and head movements.

Rick cannot talk or use his arms and legs, yet he has competed in an astounding 780 races with his father, Dick, including 55 marathons and 149 triathlons in a special racing wheelchair.

And speaking of runners, there's Tony Volpentest who was born *without hands and feet.* In order to overcome shyness and embarrassment, Tony began running in competition in high school and eventually won Gold Medals in the Paralympic Games of 1992 and 1996. He was the fastest amputee sprinter in the world at the 100-meter dash: 11.63 seconds.

Now you might recall that the world record for two-legged runners in the 100-meter dash is, at the time of this writing, 9.86 seconds; but if you think 11.63 seconds is slow, I welcome you to try it. Incidentally, his best time in the 200-meter is 23.07 seconds, also a world record for amputees.

Tony says, "Being successful at sports has given me more confidence. I'd always compared myself on a team sport level to able-bodied athletes. I'd never thought about comparing myself to disabled athletes. There were none around me."

He runs on specially-designed prostheses made of lightweight carbon graphite, and they enable him to run almost as though he has normal legs. I saw Tony in the 1996 Paralympics in Atlanta and he was phenomenal! What an inspiration!

As I read and re-read these inspirational stories, I look at myself as an Olympic athlete. I train my body and mind to perform, but not just for a short-lived sports event. I train my body and mind to perform for eight, nine or ten hours a day, every day, and I include in my daily training the words from the Olympic Oath:

Let me win,
But if I cannot win
Let me be brave in the attempt.
Faster, higher, stronger.

I especially like the story of Thomas Edison who, you may recall, had a devastating fire in his laboratory in Orange, NJ. As he was standing on the street corner watching his life's work being destroyed, a news reporter recorded this quote: "All our mistakes are burnt, we start again tomorrow!" They asked if he was discouraged after 10,000 failures while inventing the light bulb. He said, "Not at all, I have successfully found 10,000 ways the light bulb will not light."

The habit of finding benefits in adversity sometimes has its downside as well. A while back I had a date in my continuing search for a wife. This lady and I were going to dinner at one of my favorite restaurants, the Wayside Inn in Sudbury, MA. It was to be a romantic, candlelight dinner and our reservation was for 7:30, but the traffic was backed up in the center of Wayland and we were going to be late. I turned to Alice and said, "This traffic is great...now we have more time together." She rolled her eyes up to the top of her head (I think you know what that means). Later that evening she told me I was too happy for her. That was the last I saw of her. Oh, well, you can't win them all.

On a more serious note there is the wisdom of Dr. Victor Frankl, originally a psychiatrist in Vienna, who was captured and incarcerated in a concentration camp during World War II in Nazi Germany. He became one of the most influential people in my life after I read his book, *Man's Search for Meaning*, where he describes how he forced himself, and enabled others, to survive. He had been tortured, isolated and starved, and he lived every day with the probability of death as he witnessed so many of his countrymen being slaughtered.

In his book, Dr. Frankl asks: What are the stimuli in life that would force you to act? For most of us, the stimuli are not as dramatic as those experienced by him, but, nevertheless, they are very important to each of us: sickness, accidents, divorce, a death in the family, the possibility of losing a job, perhaps change of any kind—we all deal with stimuli. He goes on to say that we have control over only one thing in our lives, our thoughts, and then asks the question, are you willing to take responsibility for your thoughts and emotions in response to your stimuli?

All of these are methods that help me to develop more courage, and examples of people who have demonstrated great courage and who act as inspiration for me. Now let me list the things I believe will help, in the sequence I believe is most effective.

1) Developing a new interpretation of adversity. Remember the story of Thomas Edison? After his lab had burnt down, reporters asked if he was discouraged after 10,000 failures while inventing the light bulb. He said, "Not at all, I have successfully found 10,000 ways the light bulb will not light."

2) Confidence-building measures. You'll certainly remember my mother, who, after winning so many games with me, became so confident in her ability to play poker that she was ready to turn pro at the casino.

3) Controlling fear. A good way to control fear is by experiencing *controlled fear*, that is, deliberately placing yourself in a planned, uncomfortable environment (under safe conditions, as in my outward-bound-type groups) and gradually desensitizing yourself until the fear is either gone or manageable.

4) Visual simulation. I've talked about this extensively in previous chapters, so you already know its effectiveness. In this chapter I described how I took pictures of company logos and with them made a goals poster that helped me visualize my successful presentations.

5) Preparation. There's the example of my driving in the snow. I prepared myself mentally and physically for how I would react in a snow skid, and when it actually happened, I didn't slam on the brakes—I floored the accelerator and powered out of the skid into a straight line! Actually, for most of my goals, I *over-prepare* for important tasks I will be called upon to do, which helps build even more confidence.

6) Inspiration. There are so many wonderful stories of courage to draw on, ones that help to inspire our own courage. There's the example I gave of Burnell Wallace who, while terribly burned, forced herself to crawl for miles to safety. And Tony Volpentest, the amazing gold medalist at the Paralympics, who was born without hands and feet. And the many, many others that you and I could both name.

7) Purpose. Dr. Viktor Frankl, now deceased, was one of the most highly revered psychiatrists in the world. He developed the concept of *logotherapy,* which states that having meaning, or purpose, in life is the single most effective way to overcome adversity. By making inmates of concentration camps focus on their families and careers back home, and the possibility of returning to them, he enabled countless prisoners to survive. Courage draws strength from *purpose,* and that is why it is important to maintain awareness of purpose on a daily basis.

8) Taking responsibility for thoughts and emotions. An element of Dr. Frankl's logotherapy is that we all have the ability (whether we know it or not) to decide how we will react to circumstances. It is sometimes hard to do, but it can be done. Remember the story about young Tiger Woods, whose mother told him, "Let your clubs speak for you instead of getting upset or mad with the disqualification."? He decided that's what he would do from then on, and his fame speaks for itself.

9) Taking Action. I said earlier in this chapter that it is important to take action believing you will succeed. I have experienced countless times in my own life, and in the lives of my students, how the very act of taking action toward a goal reduces the fear of the action, itself, and of failure.

(NOTE: 98% of the people I meet have no idea what knowledge, skills or assistance are needed in order to execute and achieve a goal. They think it's spending more time on something or working harder at it. But the key to effective action is working smarter.)

10) Small steps. How many times have I been stymied by obstacles that initially seemed too big and too scary for me to overcome? And just as often, I have been able to overcome them by beginning with small, do-able steps. Instead of a note that says "Make presentation to Company X," I can break this down into simple tasks that create momentum. For example, my note might say "Research Company X, identify key decision-makers." Too big? How about "Turn on computer and locate Company X on Internet"? That's pretty easy to do as a first step. And having done an easy first step, you'll find the courage and determination to continue.

Some final thoughts on courage. I turn my weaknesses into strength, my fear into resolve, by developing a tough-minded singleness of purpose. If I should ever experience job dissatisfaction, distress or a lack of energy in my life, I now realize this is due to a lack of *purpose* or goals in my life. Two of the greatest purposes in life are family and career, and I love my family and I love my career.

I see the success I want in my imagination. This increases my intensity to achieve and develop an "I can" attitude. But I must always remember it may take one to twenty years to accomplish all my objectives.

I understand that fear is not a reason to quit; it's only an excuse. I've learned that my persistence and courage will achieve the same results as someone else who may have more talent and intellect. If I am to be a high-achiever, if I am to be successful in my goals, I have to keep moving forward when fear occurs in my life. This takes courage, real courage. But I have a date with destiny that *will not be broken;* that destiny is to become the best person I can be.

Action Steps for this chapter:

1) Ask yourself: Do you see courage as an important aspect of your future success? Are you honestly willing to work on developing more courage?

2) See if you can identify the most important purposes of your life, and write them down in order of importance. Include long-term goals for which you will need to take action in order to achieve.

3) Try to identify and list the actions that must be taken, as well as the obstacles to be overcome, in order to achieve each of these goals.

4) What might prevent you from taking the necessary actions and/or overcoming the obstacles? Of these, try to distinguish which are based upon practicality (money needed for something, the need to be in a different location, etc.) as opposed to fear (fear of meeting someone, of public speaking, of being seen as incompetent, etc.).

5) This step will take some work, but it is a good test of how serious you are about gaining the courage to achieve your goals. Review the first *eight* steps above and determine how many of these steps are relevant and useful to achieving each of your goals. *Do this for each of your goals.*

6) Finally, what actions (including small steps) can you begin *right now* that will help strengthen the courage you will need to achieve your goals?

11

ADAPTABILITY—A SELF-MANAGEMENT SKILL

Anthropologists have been studying a native tribe in South America where members have been dying prematurely of a strange malady for many generations. It was recently discovered that the disease is caused by the bite of an insect that lives in the walls of their adobe homes. The natives have several possible alternatives. They can eliminate the insects with an insecticide; they can destroy and rebuild their homes in a way that prevents infestation; they can move to another area where there are no such insects; or they can continue to live and die early, just as they have done for generations. They have chosen to remain as they are and die early.

To have a dynamic, thriving economy in the modern world, there is a need to have a highly trained and motivated work force that is flexible and adaptable to a changing market and changing technological conditions. In this modern, fast-paced, competitive world, business as usual won't work; there are going to be constant re-engineering, reorganization, job transfers, new bosses, new policies, new methods, budget cutbacks, and new locations. Flexibility and adaptability are especially necessary for high-achievers, and if I want to be a high-achiever in this modern economy I will have to accommodate them.

In my own case, in my formative years I lacked the willingness to change until the pain of changing became less than the pain of staying the same. I thought change was the worst occurrence that could happen because it made me feel uncomfortable. Change also upset my security because with change comes new challenges, and no one likes being a beginner. Like many of us, I coveted the things that are easy, fun and fast-tension-relieving; it took me many years to learn to accept the challenge of things that are hard, slow and goal-achieving.

Talk about change: I think about the changes my body has experienced since high school when I used to eat a Twinkie, a Moon Pie and a Three Musketeers in one day. Today I just think about it and I gain weight.

But change is a constant I now accept. I am aware that constant change is a part of my life, particularly on the job, because it occurs not just yearly, but monthly, weekly and sometimes even hourly! I must be prepared to embrace it.

The best way I have found to develop adaptability to change is to understand and internalize these three concepts.

The first is that my company, whichever company it is, will be frequently making prudent changes—risk-taking decisions to keep itself financially strong and capable of effectively and efficiently serving the customer. The changes may not seem beneficial to me at the time because I am interpreting the changes with limited information. This is an important point; let me repeat it.

CHANGE MAY NOT SEEM BENEFICIAL BECAUSE IT IS OFTEN INTERPRETED WITH LIMITED INFORMATION

But if I allow myself to become discouraged because of the changes, such as working longer hours, having different job responsibilities, or doing more with less, then I have created an additional challenge for myself; in addition to the actual changes, I have to deal with my discouragement.

The second concept that needs to be understood is there may be confusion and a temporary lack of productivity with change. Again, I will not allow myself to become pessimistic about the new situation but will understand that it takes time for familiarity to be gained with any change, and for the change, itself, to take effect.

ALLOW TIME FOR CHANGES TO BECOME EFFECTIVE

The third concept is that uncertainty and change are normal and to be expected. Peak performers not only anticipate change, but also reach out to embrace it before it overpowers them.

UNCERTAINTY AND CHANGE ARE NORMAL AND TO BE EXPECTED

Jack Welch, ex-CEO of General Electric, says that, "Every time there is change, there is an opportunity to get energized rather than paralyzed." Right on!

My definition of a realist is someone who has a contingency plan. I try to be that realist. I expect the best, plan in case of the worst and I am prepared for surprise, whatever happens. I program myself so that no matter what happens I'm ready to take full advantage of it. I appreciate how everything changes moment to moment. I welcome change as an opportunity and a challenge to learn, grow, and improve my productivity.

The wonderful side effect of this is that as I become more flexible and adaptable, the range of possibilities open to me increases and I have more choices. The more choices I have, the more inner freedom I feel and the more room I have for creativity. It is a win-win situation for my company and for me, personally.

Job security is a term utilized in the '80s and early '90s, but forget it. I don't need it. I now have something much more valuable. I have employability! I have value! Here is a list of the traits that are the result of being flexible and adaptable.

- I respond positively to new events and situations.
- In my quest to become the high-achiever I envision, I am fast, flexible and focused.
- I am open to ideas other than my own.
- I am always looking for better alternatives to *the way we've done it.*
- I respond positively to increases or other changes in workload by innovative thinking and planning.
- I respond to changing priorities proactively, and encourage others to respond positively.
- I prioritize multiple projects and needs, and handle multiple tasks simultaneously as needed.
- I am willing to learn new technology, processes and methods.
- I demonstrate resolve and determination in the face of setbacks.
- I look for creative ways to make the best use of limited resources.
- I remain calm and focused when confronted with high pressure.
- I am prepared to take calculated risks.
- I work cooperatively and effectively with all levels and kinds of people.
- My supervision of others is tailored to meet the individual needs of each employee.
- I engage in my own cross-training and proactively assist others to do the same.
- I understand others' fear of change, and I provide accurate information, encouragement and opportunities to others before, during and after changes.
- I encourage others to think creatively, innovatively and boldly.

Action Steps for this chapter:

1) Look at your own work situation and (being as honest as possible) list the things that frighten you (from small details to your future with the company); then list the things that cause you pain or discomfort (from small details to co-workers to company policies); then list the things that discourage you (from lack of resources, low compensation, mismanagement, etc.).

2) Now list the positive things about your work situation (strong points of co-workers, company potential and individual opportunities, satisfaction in doing a good job, etc.)

3) Based on a comparison of your points of dissatisfaction and satisfaction, rate your overall, current work situation on a scale of 1 to 10, where 1 is totally negative and 10 is totally positive.

4) Review each of the bullet points above and *assume you are already that person who is flexible and adaptable.*

5) *With this assumption strongly in mind,* go through each of your points of dissatisfaction; think about each one and, one by one, see if anything has changed.

6) In view of the above, has your overall rating of your work situation changed?

7) Having actually done all of the above action steps, how do you *now* feel about your ability to be flexible and adaptable?

12

CUSTOMER FOCUS
—A SELF-MANAGEMENT SKILL

It's a customer-focused and customer-driven business culture today. If I want to be successful in the modern economy I need to be a *go-giver* rather than a *go-getter.* Why? Because my rewards will be in proportion to my service. Service is an attitude, not a department. The purpose of business is to serve the customer—the by-product is profit. If I remember nothing else from this chapter, I must remember this:

THE PURPOSE OF BUSINESS IS TO SERVE THE CUSTOMER THE BY-PRODUCT IS PROFIT

Customer satisfaction today means not only meeting but exceeding customer expectations. *Wow* the customer! There is a furniture store in New England called Jordan's Furniture. They have only four locations in Massachusetts and New Hampshire, but they are considered the best of their kind in the country. Their mission statement is simply, "We vow to wow!"

To be successful in the 21st century, a company must be customer-driven rather than operations-driven. This is how I tell the difference.

OPERATIONS-DRIVEN BUSINESS		CUSTOMER-DRIVEN BUSINESS
Serves the *company*	ORIENTATION	Serves the *customer*
INTERNAL Consistently looks for ways to improve profits	PRIMARY FOCUS	EXTERNAL Consistently looks for ways to provide better products and service for its customers
Product features	SALES FOCUS	Customer benefits
Customer needs get in the way of efficient operation	CUSTOMER SERVICE ATTITUDE	Customers are responsible for the existence of the company
Focus on how to cut costs	REACTION TO A SALES DOWNTURN	Focus on ways to improve quality, delivery and attention to customer needs. Retain quality staff by investing in employees

Customer-focused people are double winners. They live the win/win philosophy. If I help you win, then I win. If I disagree with your viewpoint and start to argue with you, what is the result? You will argue with me, and one of us must lose; and if one loses, the relationship loses.

This reminds me of the classic story about Calvin Coolidge. Coolidge, a president of few words, was renowned for saying little and often replying with a mono-syllable (most often "hmm"). One evening a dinner guest at the White House bet another guest that she could get the president to say more than two words. Hoping for a sympathetic response, she informed the president of her wager and waited expectantly. Coolidge's response was "You lose."

Well, I believe in win-win and that making our relationships beneficial is more important than emphasizing our differences. I seek mutual benefit in all interactions and see life as a cooperative, not a competitive arena. I strongly believe in the win-win philosophy, and I know that win/win results are achieved by first learning to listen.

I SEEK FIRST TO UNDERSTAND, THEN TO BE UNDERSTOOD.

This is one of the most important keys to effective interpersonal communication. Most people listen with the intent to reply; they are only half listening, while the other half is preparing how to respond. But I want to listen with the intent to understand. I need to see the world the way my clients see the world. I need to understand *their* feelings. Effective communication is an art. Alfred Viera, a communications specialist with Business Design Associates, puts it this way: "...the words that are spoken are never sufficient to provide all the meaning that a given speaker intends to convey." So I need to listen with my eyes, ears, and heart, to understand deeply with both my intellect and my intuition.

Once I understand a client's needs, preferences and fears, then I can focus on problem-solving and selling. When a client talks to me in terms of facts, details, quantities, specifications, etc., I will respond in a similar fashion. But when I hear a client *expressing a feeling,* I immediately go back to empathetic listening; and if I am listening carefully, I can usually tell the nature of the client's feeling and address the issue appropriately.

Listening is the best way to show respect for others. Listening builds trust and cooperation and shows my understanding and concern, as well as reducing relationship tensions. The essence of empathetic listening is not that I must agree with someone but that I fully and deeply understand that person's views.

When my clients feel I understand, their defenses come down; I have given them their needed psychological space, which causes the barrier between what's actually going on inside another person and what's being communicated to me to disappear. When I deeply understand my clients, I open the door to creative solutions—I can get anything in life I want if I help enough other people get what they want. That's another powerful statement worth repeating.

I CAN GET ANYTHING IN LIFE I WANT IF I HELP ENOUGH OTHER PEOPLE GET WHAT THEY WANT

Here is a list that is used as a survey for companies to help determine to what extent they are customer-focused.* The companies are asked to rate on a sliding scale to what extent each statement applies to them.

1) Beyond understanding the routine requirements of a particular job, an employee needs to identify with some core purpose of the larger organization.

2) Individuals and teams need to receive regular feedback as to the effect of their performance on internal and external customers.

3) Customer requirements need to be recognized as principal drivers of the changes and improvements that are made in products, systems, the work culture, and day-to-day work procedures.

4) While all customers are significant, it is important to identify certain customers as "high priority" customers in terms of their potential impact on the long-term success of your organization.

5) Individuals need to incorporate the idea of being "the customer's champion" as a primary factor in their own success and career progression.

6) An organization needs to anticipate the future needs of its customers, even though these may be outside the current charter of the business.

7) Effective job performance is best acknowledged on the basis of outcomes or results produced for the customer and secondarily on the fact of "job completion" and other internal performance criteria.

8) Creative ways to say "yes" to the customer should be emphasized. The word "policy" should be limited to matters of legal compliance, ethics, or absolute performance standards such as "employee safety."

9) It is important for each employee to recognize and help manage specific situations that cause the customer to form crucial first impressions of the organization's products, procedures, and people.

10) The handling of difficult customer situations (and personalities) is a key demonstration of well-developed customer service skill and overall professionalism.

*This listing is printed here by courtesy of Darby Checketts, President of Cornerstone Professional Development, Mesa, Arizona, and author of the "Customer Astonishment Handbook."

Here are some additional specific traits that I must develop and demonstrate for effective customer focus.

♦ I make sure that I and all staff are visible and accessible to customers.
♦ I am courteous and respectful in all dealings with customers, at all times.
♦ I assume responsibility for customer concerns, and I do not pass the buck to someone else.
♦ I respond to all customer concerns by acting immediately to help them..

- I give all customers individual attention and make them feel that their problem or challenge is unique.
- I respond promptly to all customer requests for information.
- I understand that all co-workers and associates are also customers, and I treat them as such.
- I assist customers in making informed decisions.
- I design work processes that are responsive to customer needs, and I make sure these processes are customer-friendly.
- I identify and promptly correct barriers to good customer service.
- I establish fair and effective company standards for customer redress procedures.
- I am reliable; I follow through with what I say, and I act with integrity.
- I establish and maintain mechanisms for ongoing customer feedback.
- I base strategic planning on customer feedback and their projected needs.

One of my goals is excellence in business. I understand that my advancement, recognition and continual employment are directly related to my contribution. I'm constantly searching for ways to improve my efficiency and contribution through *empowered excellence*. I test the limits of my contribution; that is, I willingly do more than I'm paid to do, with a pleasing mental attitude. I'm multi-task oriented.

I have eliminated the statement, "That's not my job." When I work forty hours, I'm working to survive. When I work forty-plus hours, I'm working for success. I exercise my privilege to go the extra mile. Why? So I can make an investment in my future!

Some people say, "I believe I'm giving too much, but not getting." But in truth I can never give too much. My getting is in direct proportion to my giving. I know I will receive even though it may not be now or next week, but

I will receive. It is the law! It may take one year or five years, but I will receive. I never ask what my manager or company can do for me. I ask what I can do for my company. Abraham Lincoln's quote is appropriate: "If you're too big a person to do a little job, then you're too little a person to do a big job."

Much of this is taken for granted. We sometimes assume that customer-focus is a natural and automatic manifestation of our business practice. But there is a tendency for each of us to slide back into placing priority on the internal details of our jobs and to forget who ultimately pays the bills. That is why I frequently review all of the above. As I said in the beginning of this chapter, being a *go-giver* is more important than being a *go-getter*. I am going to be very successful in the 21st century, and this is one of the things that will make it happen.

Action Steps for this chapter:

1) Review the operations-driven vs. customer-driven chart above and evaluate which priority your present company exhibits.

2) Take the above ten-point survey, based on your company, and rate on a scale of 1 to 10 to what extent each point applies to it.

3) Review the 13 traits described above and evaluate to what extent they apply to you personally.

4) Given your present position, are there any steps you can take to influence the customer orientation of your company?

5) Given your present position, what steps can you take to improve your own customer-focus orientation?

13

RELATIONSHIPS AND SYNERGY
—SELF-MANAGEMENT SKILLS

Here is a charming true story, related by an associate, that I would like to share with you.

"I grew up in Chicago during the years of World War II. Lots of things were scarce then and food was rationed. But in the midst of these scarcities, our family was well off because my father had a wholesale food business and we were able to get just about everything edible (including the greatest of rarities during WWII—bubble gum!). Everyone liked my dad, he had friends everywhere, and he knew how to treat them. I got a good glimpse of that one day, as well as how the city of Chicago worked.

"I was riding in my dad's truck, helping to deliver some "wheels" of hard-to-get Wisconsin cheddar cheese to restaurants. Have you ever seen a wheel of cheese? It's a solid chunk, about the size and shape of a large car tire, and weighs 40-80 lbs. That day we were delivering them to a posh restaurant in the downtown section of Chicago known as "The Loop." Even in the '40s, The Loop was a very crowded area, and it was almost impossible to find a parking place. At that time, all of the downtown traffic police rode horses, and they spent most of their time handing out parking tickets to the many illegally parked cars and trucks.

"My dad stopped our truck alongside the parked cars in front of a restaurant and, before making the delivery, he took out a large knife, cut a wedge out of one of the cheese wheels, and wrapped it up (in waxed paper—there was no plastic then). That single wedge was about a foot and a half long, and, by itself, weighed maybe 15 lbs. My dad told me it was for one of the cops (that's what they called themselves—never "policemen" or "peace officers") who was having a hard time making ends meet. This particular cop had a big family to feed, and 15 lbs. of Wisconsin cheddar, a tightly rationed item, was a treasure.

"A moment later I heard the sharp clip-clop of hooves on pavement, and a burly, middle-aged cop came up to our truck and leaned over into the cab. He called out, "Hi, Carl, hawaya? That your sonny boy with you?" I waved to the cop and, after the mutual inquiries about families were over, my dad said, "Mike, I'm overloaded with too much cheese this week and it's only going to waste. Could you help me by taking some off my hands?" and he handed over that big wedge of cheese. You should have seen that cop's eyes light up when he saw it. He grinned, and stuck the cheese into his saddlebag, two-thirds of it sticking out like a bright orange tower. After thanking my dad, the cop asked, "Delivering today, Carl?" My dad told him yes, and the cop said, "Just double-park here and I'll watch things for you." I helped my dad carry in two cheese wheels to the restaurant, and when we came back outside, there was the cop, seated on his tall, brown horse, holding up a line of traffic until my Dad could move our truck out of the way.

"It wasn't bribery or payoff—I sensed the cop would have helped my dad even without the gift of cheese—it was a way of greasing the wheels of commerce, and of ordinary folks looking after each other whenever they could. But even as a boy, I was impressed by my father's thoughtfulness, not merely by giving, but in the way he had given so that the cop lost no dignity in receiving.

"Among the working people that was how Chicago operated in those days; people helping people and working together to make a thriving, vibrant metropolis."

In the previous chapter I talked about listening to clients and doing my best to understand them. But, in fact, not only clients, but everyone I deal with and depend upon every day is a kind of customer because they all affect my potential success. The secretary who types and mails my correspondence; the mechanic who makes sure my car is running okay; the grocer who provides me with safe and healthy food; all are my customers in the sense that I need something from them, and they need something from me. So I want to be able to really understand everyone I know and have dealings with. But there are some obstacles. Here are some thoughts on biases and perceptions.

When North Americans are asked to describe what they see in the drawing above, most say a house with a window, and an adult and two children standing beside it. However, when people in rural Kenya are shown the same drawing, they describe it as two children with a woman on her way to market, carrying a package on her head, walking by a tree that has been denuded by elephants and giraffes. As soon as this Kenyan impression is mentioned to us, we can see the situation through the eyes of the Kenyans. Similarly, if the Kenyans have been to a city or town with rectangular buildings and windows, and we explain our interpretation to them, they are also able to see it through our eyes.

In recent years a new understanding of communication has come about which is very powerful. I'll see if I can summarize this briefly. For thousands of years, human beings have used language in a certain way. Linguists call it *representationalism*. What this means is that when we want to convey information to someone else, all we have to do is to speak clearly enough and the recipient will understand the information exactly as we have understood it. In this view, if our words are carefully chosen, they are like a telephone wire that passes the signal from speaker to listener without alteration.

This type of communication is sometimes called the accounting view of language. It assumes there is an objective truth out there just waiting to be explained to someone else. It also assumes that a listener is "right" only if he understands the message in exactly the same way as the speaker, and he is "wrong" if he understands any part of it differently. Thus begin the age-old battles of who is "right" and who is "wrong."

While this understanding of communication has served us fairly well in the past, it has also led to much miscommunication and trouble. It enables one or more persons to claim ownership of the "truth," and that there can only be one truth. This precludes any meaningful dialog.

But in recent years linguists have described a new understanding of communication; they call it the *generative view of language.* In this view, all information, descriptions, events and stories are altered through our individual filters of culture, history, personal background and mood. We each create our own version of what is "right." In fact, through this view of communication, we are all "right."

Now there are circumstances where *representationalism* is necessary. If we are building a bridge, we all have to get the specs correct or the bridge will fail. But if we are interested in human needs, motivation, desires and goals, *generative* communication has practical benefits. For one, it is future-oriented. Instead of emphasis being placed on who is right and who is wrong, this view of communication asks, "How will my understanding of this conversation and your understanding of it shape my future and your future? Will this conversation help us to generate common action?"

When we learn to communicate in this way, new vistas open up, new avenues are seen. So learning to be aware of our differing perceptions isn't just idle entertainment—it helps build compromise, mutual understanding and trust. When persons have had some experience in understanding the differing perceptions of others, the next time there is a conflict they are better prepared for resolution.

(From the book *For Love & Money* by Roy O. Williams. Reprinted courtesy of Monterey Pacific Publishing)

This is great stuff. Why is it so difficult for so many people to do? In recent years psychologists have focused increasingly on what they call EQ, *emotional intelligence,* the capacity to control our own emotions, to correctly identify those of others, and to guide our relationships based on this knowledge. In studies done of leadership, researchers have found that the higher the position, the more EQ is the determining factor of success. It is not that EQ takes the place of logical intelligence; all successful leaders must also have intellectual ability. It's that leaders can vary in their degree of logical intelligence, but the presence of a significant degree of EQ is absolutely essential to success.

I try to employ EQ whenever possible. For example, no one wins an argument, someone always loses. Adversarial relationships are counterproductive and outmoded. If I win an argument I may temporarily feel smug, but what has it done for our relationship?

Instead I value the differences between myself and others. When someone disagrees with me, I first seek to understand where he or she is coming from. Then I try to affirm the legitimacy of the other person's view. When I really understand, I think "If I were you I would feel the same way," because I treat others the same way I treat me.

Like everyone else, I prefer to be accepted, but I don't need it. It's not necessary that others accept me. This eliminates my discouragement from receiving negative responses. When people say "no" to me or someone is disagreeable or offensive toward me, I am non-judgmental, non-interpretative, and non-evaluative. I understand and accept the emotions of those who may wrong me, and because I understand, I am forgiving and accepting of them. Here is an important precept for me to remember: to accept requires no effort; to resist requires effort; if resentment is involved it requires the continuing expenditure of energy. Acceptance, therefore, is a way to keep my energy high and stay focused on my goals.

When I deeply understand and accept other people's views, I open the door to creative solutions. Our differences are no longer stumbling blocks to communication and progress. Instead our differences become the stepping stones to synergy.

Synergy is the principle of creative cooperation. It states that the cooperative whole is greater than the sum of our individual selves. Thus the essence of synergy is to value differences, to respect them, to build on our strengths and compensate for our weaknesses. The key to valuing differences is to realize that all people see the world not as it is, but as *they* are! To be successful, I must value differences in people because those differences not only add to my knowledge, they create the whole that is greater then its individual parts—us!

A cooperative environment stimulates creativity and peak performance. We need to break down barriers between people by developing strategies for increasing cooperation.

THE COOPERATIVE WHOLE IS GREATER THAN THE SUM OF OUR INDIVIDUAL SELVES

So how shall I go about building this cooperative whole? How do I develop this synergy? Teddy Roosevelt said it accurately in the following quotation: "It is not the critic who counts, not the man/woman who points out how the strong man/woman has stumbled, or where the doer of deeds could have done them better. The credit belongs to the man/woman who is actually in the arena; whose face is marred by the dust, sweat, blood, who strives valiantly, who errs and comes short again and again, who knows the great enthusiasms, the great devotions and spends himself/herself in a worthy cause, and who at best knows in the end the triumph of high achievement, and who at worst, if he/she fails, at least fails while daring greatly."

I will start by treating people the way they want to be treated. I will not criticize, condemn or complain. Criticism of performers doesn't aid the performance. People who say it can't be done should not interrupt those who are doing it. If I find it necessary to correct someone to improve their performance in order to help them to learn, then I will at the same time criticize their behavior (in a solution-oriented, non-blaming way) and encourage the person.

I encourage people to *charge on,* which reminds me of the story about Arnold Palmer. Arnold Palmer was, of course, a great champion golfer, but one year he hadn't yet won a tournament. That day he was playing in a tournament but was not leading the pack when he heard someone shouting from the gallery. Each time as Arnie would select his golf club, he could hear the shouted words, "Charge on, Arnie, you can do it! Charge on!" Well, he went on to win the tournament, perhaps with the help of this inspiration. At the end he went to the audience and asked, "Who was screaming *charge on?*" A gentleman raised his hand. Arnie thanked him and reached out to shake his hand to introduce himself. However, the gentleman didn't respond. Instead he said to Arnie, "You and I are world famous golfers. I'm Charlie Boswell, and I've always had a dream to play golf with you for $1,000 a hole." Arnie replied, "I'm sorry, I don't know you." Charlie said, "I'm Charlie Boswell, the blind golfing champion of the world." So Arnie said, half in jest, "Sure I'll play $1,000 dollars a hole. When do you want to play?" Charlie said, "Any night!"

When I'm in a position where I want to improve people's performance I use the *sandwich technique,* or a modification of it. I encourage them to charge on. First I praise them for something they are doing well. Then I offer *constructive* criticism to them by saying something like "I know you can do better than that. How about trying it this way?" Then I praise them again. When I leave them with praise, they're thinking about their behavior and not feeling resentment for being criticized. Praising people encourages them; it gives them a mental lift and confidence.

Have you noticed that the time someone receives the most praise is at his or her wake? I don't want to wait that long. I want to do it now!

If I notice people doing something right, I reward them with praise. My praise is immediate and specific; I share my feelings and encourage them to do it again. When the praise is immediate and specific it is much more effective than if I wait and do it later, or if my praise is vague. I synergize by talking behind my colleagues' backs *positively*. If I work for someone, I need to work *for* him or her. I need to speak well of him or her and stand by the institution he or she represents. If I am so much at odds with a supervisor I should resign my position, and when I am out of the organization, then I can criticize to my heart's content. But as long as I am part of an organization, I will not condemn it. If I do, the first high wind that comes along will blow me away. And I probably won't even know why.

Philosophers, psychologists and many others have long debated to what extent altruistic actions are really selfish ones. If I do something beneficial for you, is it really for you or does it just make me feel good? There is no clear answer to this, but I am keenly aware that my own success depends to a large extent on others. So for pragmatic as well as moral and ethical reasons, when I deal with others I will invoke a new Golden Rule and treat others as *they* wish to be treated. I will be helpful, cooperative and loyal. I will avoid win-lose arguments and seek win-win situations wherever possible. On a day-to-day and moment-to-moment basis I will practice the art of synergy. And if I am able to help others as I progress toward my goals, then my success will be doubly satisfying.

Action Steps for This Chapter:

1) As you review the material in this book, be sure to review the section above on *representationalism* and *generative communication*. Then look closely at how you typically communicate. Which kind of communication do you use? Are there any changes in your communication style that might be beneficial and promote synergy?

2) Find something good that five of your colleagues or others have done each day, and be aggressive in praise.

3) Review the above section on the *sandwich technique* and try using it the next time you want to change someone's behavior or process.

4) Be aware of how you offer praise to others. Is your praise specific and is it immediate (in the "now" rather than referring to something in the past)?

5) Be totally honest with yourself. Do you believe that you help yourself by helping others? If yes, are you ready to apply this to *everything* you do in your professional life?

14

ASSOCIATING WITH WINNERS
—A SELF-MANAGEMENT SKILL

Have you heard the one about the bank robber in San Francisco? He walked into the downtown branch of Bank of America, stopped at one of the forms counters, picked up a withdrawal slip and wrote on it, "This is a stickup. Give me all your money." The bank was crowded so he got into a teller line and waited for his turn. But as he waited he thought someone might have seen him writing the note. So he left Bank of America and walked across the street to the Wells Fargo bank. The line was short there, and after a few moments he handed his form to the Wells Fargo teller. She boldly told him she could not accept the form because it was written on a Bank of America withdrawal slip, and that he would either have to fill out a Wells Fargo form or go back to Bank of America. The man looked confused for a moment, then he said "okay" and left. He crossed the street again and entered Bank of America. Meanwhile, someone at Wells Fargo had alerted the police, and as he got into line once again he was arrested.

Morals and lawbreaking aside, this man was a loser. And while very few among us turn to bank robbery, many people are unsuccessful in other ways. Just thinking about losing can turn you into a loser. For example, faculty members at medical schools will tell you that something like

two-thirds of all medical students develop the symptoms of
the disease they study.

Imagine a meeting of losers. What do they talk about?
What bright, new ideas do they discuss? Do they impart
high levels of confidence? Do they inspire each other with
initiative? I don't think so. Now I have real sympathy for
the downtrodden and all the other losers among us, and in
terms of charity and volunteer work I do as much as I possibly can to help them. But in terms of pursuing personal
success, I have learned an important point over the years.

ASSOCIATE WITH WINNERS!!!

Customers like being with winners. Winners exude
confidence and an aura of success that is catching. And
winners attract winners. I'm sure you've witnessed many
occasions where successful people meet with each other—
in business, in politics, in show business, etc.—but not too
many occasions where the very successful are meeting
with the underside of society.

Then there is motivation. How do I become highly
motivated to succeed? How do I stay motivated? Having
read all of the previous chapters, you already know how I
use CPI (continuous performance improvement) in many
forms. But in addition to this, a terrific way to get motivated is to associate with winners, to listen and learn from
them.

And who do *you* hang out with? What kind of people
do *you* do business with? How are they affecting you? Are
you energized, more knowledgeable and inspired by your
professional and personal relationships? Do you come
away from your meetings with them more determined to
reach your goals? Your answers to these questions can
have a huge impact on your motivation.

Obviously, not all of our relationships have to do with
professional success. Some are old friends, some are people
we just like to have a fun, relaxing time with, etc. But even
these kinds of relationships can have a positive or negative

impact on our goals. One thing I am certain of: if a relationship results in frequent arguments that are upsetting; if a relationship results in my becoming discouraged or depressed; if a relationship results in my losing confidence and self-esteem; or if a relationship causes me to put aside my goals for any reason, then that relationship is a lose-lose one—it will not benefit any of the people involved.

How do I find successful people to associate with? Well, as a first step I use an affirmation which I repeat daily:

I HAVE MUCH TO CONTRIBUTE, AND THE PEOPLE I SEEK ARE EVEN NOW SEEKING ME

Then I set my sights on connecting with people who are very successful in their field. I could name hundreds of highly successful people I have worked with. Here are a few examples.

I remember meeting with Gary Moulton, Peter Napoli and Bob McDougal, who together run the largest and most successful owner-operated McDonald's franchise in the world—Colley/McCoy, with seventy-nine restaurants today. When I called for an appointment with Gary Moulton, I asked if we could meet at one of their McDonald's. I felt that I couldn't lose in an atmosphere where excellence in policy and practice was the order of the day.

Gary took me on a tour of the facility, including the kitchen and storage areas. That impression was imprinted on my mind forever. It was spotless, pristine and well-organized. Gary asked if I would like a Filet Sandwich, and I said yes and bit into it. Well, he was setting me up. The sandwich was mushy. "Richard," he said, " this was out on the rack for more than ten minutes." He took it out of my hand and threw it in the trash. Then he gave me one that had been out for only one minute. It was terrific! It was that delicious, consistent taste that I expected. "Richard," Gary said, "see the difference attention to detail makes." That's one of the reasons for their success. If it didn't meet Colley/McCoy's high standards, they threw it away.

Whenever I go into a McDonald's I imagine myself in a magical place where anything is possible. I get my inspiration not just from eating a sandwich and fries and a coke—but from my association with great customer service, consistent high quality food and sharp, competent business acumen.

Wes Elmer is the president of Coca-Cola of Northern New England. His Coca-Cola facility is recognized as one of the best in the world. Wes told me one day that his company had won the President's Trophy for quality control seven out of the last nine years; that's like winning the Super Bowl seven times in nine years! Some people dream success but Wes lives it daily.

Ted Highberger, former president of Coca-Cola of New England, is another good example. Back in 1986 I shared one of my dreams and asked him to sponsor my Leadership Programs for teachers and teenagers. He did, and my heart filled with joy. It is important to me that some company like Coca-Cola or McDonald's sponsor me because they are prototypes of excellence. And if I teach excellence, then I want to be sponsored by a company that lives excellence.

I have had approximately 8,000 McDonald's employees graduate from my program. For every dollar Coca-Cola has spent on me, I am able to give back $100 in increased productivity and profits, and to realize this benefit not in some distant future but within thirty days! I see the Coca-Cola Company as a winner, and they see me the same way. Winners associate with winners.

I deeply love training McDonald's and Coca-Cola employees. I imagine myself as their coach and them as Olympic athletes who are the best in the world. Why are they the best? They work hard and smart. Please let me say it again. They work very hard and very smart. Becoming the largest in the world is one thing, but maintaining it year after year—that's awesome.

As a presenter to many diverse corporations, I get the chance to meet people who can give me practical knowledge as well as the wisdom of how to use it. In my own mind, I create so many ideas that I need a sounding board to determine if these ideas are based on reality or unrealistic. My sounding board is other winners, and I work hard to keep my associations.

Once you have established good relations with other winners, here are four basic points to remember in order to keep the relationships sound.

1) Show up. In other words, be dependable and reliable and prompt.

2) When you commit to doing something, do it! Always!

3) Pay close attention to the needs of others, and how you might be able to help.

4) Keep the quality high. Do the very best you can, and do it consistently.

Action Steps for this chapter:

1) Make a list of the people you associate with regularly, on a business or personal basis. For each one, write down how that person affects you in terms of a) your energy level, b) your self-confidence, c) your sense of well-being, d) your knowledge, e) your enthusiasm and determination to achieve your goals, and f) your *ability* to achieve your goals.

2) Which of the above persons would you classify as "winners"? Do you see a correlation between those persons you perceive as winners and those who are beneficial to you? In terms of your goals, would you like to develop closer relations with any of the above persons? Similarly, do you believe any of the above persons are detrimental to your goals?

3) There are four points given above for helping to establish and maintain good relationships with winners. For those beneficial persons with whom you want to either establish or maintain better relations, are you presently acting in accordance with the four points? If not, are you willing to begin doing so?

15

THE HIGH ROAD
—A SELF-MANAGEMENT SKILL

Ralph Waldo Emerson's essay "The Law of Compensation" taught me how to earn more money. It says that, "The money I'm paid by my company is in direct proportion to the need for what I do, my ability to do it, and the degree of difficulty involved in replacing me."

Very true, and we would all do well to heed this. But there is another important factor involved in my long-term success, a factor you already know. It has been said many times by many others, yet I believe it bears repeating.

In spite of the many wonderful, competent people involved in the world of business, our culture sometimes exhibits a creeping tendency to neglect ethics in the pursuit of maximizing short-term gain. We have all experienced situations where a profit can be made by ignoring the ethics of the deal. And this becomes even more compelling in lean times.

But anyone who has dealt with the business world over the long term knows the necessity of choosing the High Road—the road of ethics, integrity and generosity.

In my own experience, I have found that the world of commerce is directly related to the spiritual laws that govern our lives. For example, I know that my actions will attract like actions back to me. If I should take advantage of others, the world will respond by providing me with ample opportunities to harm myself. And if I help others, I, too, will receive help, often from unexpected sources.

Further, I believe there is an ethical system that exists throughout the world—call it what you will—that somehow responds not only to what we do but to our thoughts as well. From my own experience I know that my success is related to the degree I am in harmony with this ethical system; and that I am most in harmony with it when I follow my sense of what is right, and avoid doing what I know is wrong.

If you have been involved with the world of commerce for any length of time, you know that this is not something you learn in school; it comes from years of being faced with difficult choices and then living with them. I believe that this ability to weigh all the facts, make judgments, strike balances and act in accordance with what is right is what we call wisdom. My purpose here is not to teach you anything new in this regard, but on your pathway to high achievement, to add my bit of encouragement for you to actively engage your own wisdom—to take the High Road.

16

FAITH—A SELF-MANAGEMENT QUALITY

A railroad employee was inspecting a refrigerator car and accidentally locked himself in. He was unable to get out and he shouted over and over for help, but no one heard him. After a while he gave up, accepted his fate, and decided to scratch on the walls of the car the details of his death.

Gradually, he felt his body becoming numb and wrote how he was becoming colder and colder. Then he recorded that all sensation was departing and it was hard to remain awake. Later he wrote that he could feel death approaching and that these would be his last words.

They were. Shortly thereafter the car was opened and his lifeless body was discovered. But the temperature in the car had only been 56°, there was adequate air, and he had been in the car only a few hours.

Anatoly Sharansky, former Soviet era dissident and now Deputy Prime Minister of Israel, speaks of his years spent as a prisoner in a Soviet gulag. The gulag officers and guards constantly tried to justify their own behavior and break the spirit of the prisoners by trying to convince them why their incarceration and harsh treatment were justified. They used all manner of arguments to do this: the prisoners were the parasites of society; all they wanted was disorder and chaos; they were scum who did not appreciate all the Soviet Union had done for them; and so on.

Sharansky's captors had all the advantages. In addition to weapons, they had good food, good health, warm clothing, news of the outside world and the ability to punish prisoners indiscriminately, which they did. Many of the inmates succumbed, and others, in order to get a scrap of food or a piece of clothing to avoid frostbite, admitted that they were indeed guilty and deserving of punishment.

Sharansky watched the KGB break the spirit of his fellow prisoners. When this happened, they began to weaken and die—their will to live had been broken.

There was only one way to survive; whatever hardships and rational arguments the KGB used to break his spirit, he had to cling to his faith in himself, his belief that he was right and the KGB and its tormentor guards were wrong!

The above are examples of Faith or lack of it. But what is this thing we call Faith, and how can we use it to the greatest benefit? Faith is something we believe in, and it has been an essential part of our nature since the first human walked the earth.

A faithless person depends on an objective evaluation of events and circumstances, and all future possibilities are based upon this evaluation. But if everyone acted on the fact that the odds of becoming a champion golfer or a famous movie star are thousands to one against, few would ever try to attain these goals. If in my own professional life I should be rejected twenty times in a row, do I bow to the logic that I will never again win a sale? Should I allow past objective reality to determine my course of action?

In contrast, a person who has Faith is not so buffeted by the ups and downs of reality. If I have Faith in myself, I can steer a straight course toward my goals *regardless of what actually happens*. Faith in myself gives me direction and purpose that is lacking in the faithless. If I believe in nothing, I question everything, and my goals are just transient ideas, prone to change with every new direction that the wind blows.

If I have Faith in myself, does that mean that I have to ignore information and knowledge? Not at all. If I learn, for example, that a certain company favors a certain kind of presentation, I'll certainly take that into account. Or if I learn that a certain company is a hard nut to crack, I'll take that into account, too, but it won't scare me off—I'll just work harder.

Some philosophers define Faith as a state of mind that leads people to believe something in the total absence of supporting evidence. But that is a very narrow definition. In my Faith, I will try to obtain all the supporting evidence I possibly can. In fact, I will do careful probability assessments for each of my goals and plan my strategy, using everything I have learned. *But if I have firmly decided on a goal, then I will act in pursuit of that goal regardless of the supporting evidence.*

I must have Faith in myself, in my product, my service, my company, in the success techniques I present, and in my ability to achieve what I imagine. When my mental attitude is free from fear, worry, self-doubt, and skepticism, and thoughts are directed toward what I want to achieve, that's Faith.

In previous chapters I used the acronym *SSAFBD,* which stands for *SAY IT, SEE IT, ACT IT, FEEL IT, BECOME IT—AND DO IT!* Without Faith, I can say it, I can see it in my imagination, and I can act it. But I need some degree of Faith to really, really feel it! And if I really, really feel it, I can become it and do it! So, in addition to all the other factors that I have described in previous chapters, a degree of Faith is an important component of success.

My Faith occurs in two stages. The first stage is the most crucial. It is called the *nesting stage.* This is where my ideas and dreams are planted. Then, when I begin receiving feedback about an idea from others, I have to be careful not to be a SNIOP—*susceptible to the negative influences of other people.*

I'm aware of those people who view the world darkly, seeing little sense in setting goals. "What's the point?" they ask. "Nothing works out anyway." If I should have feelings of sadness, frustration or anger, I immediately look at the flip side. For example, if I find myself thinking, "Why should I sign up for the training course, they'll never give me the promotion," I can alter my thought to "I'm going to do everything I can to get the promotion I want. I may not get it, but I'll have a better chance if I take the course; and either way I'll be a more knowledgeable person and a more valuable employee"

I must always remember, "I can if I think I can."

> If I think I am beaten, I am.
> If I think I dare not, I won't.
> Success begins with my own will.
> It's all in my state of mind.
> Life's battles are not always won
> By those who are stronger or faster.
> Sooner or later the person who wins
> Is the one who believes he or she can!

I call the second stage of Faith the *cresting stage*. This is the point where my determination of purpose is strong enough that I am strengthened and committed to attain my goal. At this stage I know that whatever the situation or challenge, I will find a way to meet it.

There is another important benefit of Faith. When I have faith in myself, it causes me to have mastery over myself. Let me emphasize the *self* part of myself, for when I have Faith in my *self* it is not *what* I achieve that brings me happiness but *who I become*. And if my Faith is strong, I not only progress toward my goal, I become an honest, loyal, trusting, trustworthy, respectful, loving, giving and caring human being. *Through Faith I have become the person I imagined myself to be.*

All of the processes and skills mentioned in the previous chapters are Faith accumulators. Whatever I vividly imagine adds to my faith in my success; what I consistently say to myself does likewise; so does ardent desire, right habits, acting as if goals are already achieved, enthusiasm, adaptability, courage, positive relationships, associating with winners, integrity, and all the other elements I have described.

I began this chapter by offering a definition of Faith as a state of mind that leads people to believe something in the total absence of supporting evidence. Then I modified that by saying, in my own case I will try to obtain all the supporting evidence I possibly can, I will do careful probability assessments for each of my goals, and I will plan my strategy using everything I have learned. And then I said, *But if I have firmly decided on a goal, then I will act in pursuit of that goal regardless of the supporting evidence.*

In the end, Faith and will and action are closely intertwined. If you are strong in your belief in yourself and your own success, that's wonderful. If you are still a bit shaky, still having doubts, don't worry, it's okay. Your task is to proceed *as if you had no doubts.* For if you act in pursuit of your goals regardless of the supporting evidence, your success is assured.

17

COMMITMENT
—A SELF-MANAGEMENT SKILL

There was an accident. His dog had been in the car with him. So it was with some surprise that he now found himself walking along a country road with his faithful companion of many years. It felt good, strolling without hurry, and he wondered where the road would take them.

After a while he noticed in the distance what looked to be a large, elaborate gate. As they drew closer, the man saw that it gleamed in the sunlight as though made of some luminescent, pearl-like material, and was surrounded on either side by a tall fence. Inside the gate, a road, seemingly paved with gold, led off into the distance. Just inside the gate a man, dressed in a long, white robe, sat on a stool behind a small desk.

The traveler and his dog walked over to the gate, and the man said, "Excuse me, but what is this place?"

The gatekeeper responded with, "Why, this is heaven."

"That's wonderful," the man said, "may we come in?"

"You may enter, sir, but I'm afraid pets aren't allowed." Then the gatekeeper unlocked the gate and began to open it.

The traveler's face saddened, and he was quiet for a moment. Then he said, "Thank you just the same," and he and his dog turned away and continued walking down the road.

After a while he noticed an old farm gate at the side of the road. The gate was open and unattended. As they drew near the man saw that there was a pleasant orchard inside, and a farmer was pruning branches.

"Hi, there," the man called.

The farmer looked up and responded with a friendly wave.

"Excuse me," the man said, "can you tell me where we are?"

"Sure," the farmer said. "This is heaven."

"Well, that's strange," said the man, "the gatekeeper at that place down the road...he said that was heaven."

"Is that the place with the big, pearly gate and the gold road?"

"Yes, that's it."

"No," the farmer said, "that's Hell."

The man replied, "Really? But they're using your name. Doesn't that bother you?"

"Not at all," the farmer said, "we're glad that they take all the folks who'd leave their best friends behind."

Of course it's just a story, but think about it. A man passed up the chance to enter heaven out of loyalty and commitment to his dog. What a sacrifice! And yet in one sense his commitment, great as it was, was made easier by the fact that it didn't last very long; he soon found the real heaven and wasn't faced with the day-after-day temptations of life.

We all know it is much easier to make a commitment than to keep one. We make a commitment out of a simple desire to accomplish something, but then we are buffeted by counter-desires caused by bodily demands, actual or imagined obstacles, distractions or just plain laziness. So what causes someone to really, really keep a commitment? Sometimes it's fear. For example, if you are told you'll die unless you change some habit *right now*, there's a good chance you'll be frightened into a strong commitment. And sometimes we become so excited, so inspired by a positive idea or a process that we make a commitment *at that time,* but it is harder to stick to it on a day-to-day basis, when the initial excitement has passed.

If our lives or our livelihood (income, shelter, food, etc.) are not directly threatened, what kind of mental state does it take for us to make and keep a firm commitment? In my early years, how many of them did I make and then break? Commitments in the form of school work, eating habits, exercise, savings, household tasks that needed doing, letters that needed writing, books that needed reading, people that needed comforting, family members that needed visiting, worthwhile donations I somehow never got around to making, and a host of others.

If I failed in my commitments to others, their disappointment hurt, and I felt badly...although not badly enough to change my behavior. With my commitments to myself, I just shrugged off the failures with an "Oh, well..." But as I matured I began to relate my commitments to something else—my self-respect. I began to understand that every time I failed to follow through in a commitment, I was not only letting other people down, I was insulting myself as well. It felt like a voice saying to me, *"Richard, how can you justify your lack of integrity to yourself?"* And I began to listen to that voice and to honor my commitments.

I no longer deprive myself of personal integrity. Now, my word is my bond, whether to others or to myself. What I say I will do, I do. No if's, and's, or but's, no excuses, no rationalizations, no extenuating circumstances, no putting it off. I take to heart the saying, *If not me, who? If not now, when?* (paraphrased words of Rabbi Hillel, the great Jewish scholar who lived around the time of Jesus).

So I am personally absolutely, totally, completely and forever committed to the processes for high achievement I have described in this book. Nevertheless, everyone has a different path to commitment, and if I am to influence others to make a commitment, I have to understand what leads them to do it and sustain it, and what transpires to break it.

Psychologists and philosophers have debated this for millennia. But it seems to me we all have do-it switches in our brains. Those switches can be tickled by fear, excitement, intellectual reasoning or any number of things. But for all of that, for a commitment to hold there must come a point when each of our switches is not just tickled but turned ON. And the nature of our switches is that once they are turned on, they cannot be turned off. It is a point when we say to ourselves, "Enough!" or "Yes!" or "No!" and we say it in such a way that it is...irrevocable.

In my seminars that describe these high-achievement procedures, the participants get so excited, so inspired and so determined that at several points they spontaneously stand up and cheer at the tops of their voices—really. By the end of the seminar their switches have been turned ON; they are ready to commit and there is no turning back. Further, many of my students have read my written materials, watched my videos and/or listened to my audio tapes EVERY SINGLE DAY for years, without missing a day! Imagine that! What a commitment!

But what I am asking you to do is a much more modest commitment. If you believe in the value of what I have described in this book; if you believe that it can place *you* on the road to high achievement; if you are really serious about attaining your goals; are you willing to try these procedures for 30 days? It is not an earth-shattering decision, nor are you having to give up entry into heaven for the sake of your dog.

In Chapter 5, I described in detail the process called CPI3030 (Continuous Performance Improvement, 30 minutes a day for 30 days). I explained why regular repetition is so important and why a minimum of 30 days is necessary to effect permanent change. The next chapter is a summary of the most important points in this book, but if you have any doubts about the efficacy of CPI3030, I recommend you go back and re-read Chapter 5.

Over the years I have tried many other systems of self-improvement, and it is my honest belief that nothing else even comes close! One of the greatest pleasures of my life is to watch my students become high-achievers and attain a degree of success they have previously only dreamt about. I cannot adequately describe the improved confidence, the development of positive habits, the enhanced self-esteem, the creativity, the increased energy, the new-found enthusiasm and the wonderful sense of purpose and accomplishment you will feel at the end of 30 days of doing these procedures.

I wish I could meet with you personally to share these ideas. But I shall have to be satisfied with tickling your commitment switch...enough to get you started and keep you going for 30 days. After that it will be up to you.

This marvelous world is waiting for you. I hope you will not disappoint it.

18

A Summary of Self-Management Knowledge, Skills and Action Steps

1) Some of us already know what we *should* do in order to become high-achievers. And if we did everything we know we *should* do, all the time, there would be no need for self-development systems. But in spite of our best intentions we all tend to forget; *out of sight, out of mind.* So a good starting point is for you to acknowledge the need for formal reminders; a system to keep yourself plugged in and moving in the direction of your goals.

2) At this point you know that your conscious mind (judge) has caused your subconscious mind (robot) to record everything you have ever said, seen, thought or felt. And because of past experiences, your robot keeps telling your judge that you are limited in what you can accomplish. Therefore, you need to re-program your robot, and the way to do that is by consciously changing what you say, see, think and feel.

3) For almost all of us, being mentally proactive is a distinct change from our former behavior in which thoughts, feelings and pictures just float into and out of our minds without our having any control over them. So this is a reminder that you are undertaking something new and different; *for a part of each day you will be thinking intentionally*!

4) You have learned that the more *clearly* you imagine your success, the more strongly it will be imprinted in your robot. Remember, $V \times I = R$ is for vividness × imagination = reality.

5) You have been given enough examples that I hope by now you are convinced that high-achievers *imagine* their accomplishments in advance—winners simulate winning—and you must now begin doing the same.

6) How we begin and end our days has an important effect on the impressions that are recorded in our subconscious robot, which is the controlling factor for our future behavior. So pay attention to the positivity or negativity with which you awaken and go to sleep.

7) When you begin to actively re-program yourself, there is a very powerful progression—*SSAFBD*. When you *say* to yourself that you are a highly effective leader, it is multiplied when you also *see* yourself as highly successful; as you *act* like it has already happened; as you *feel* yourself as successful; as you mentally *become* that successful person; and lastly, from all of the previous behaviors, you will spontaneously *do* the inevitable, resulting actions that will lead you to being that successful person in fact.

8) CPI3030. To be effective and create the changes in you that I have indicated, you must do Continuous Performance Improvement. You must spend at least 30 minutes each day performing the exercises described in this book, and you must do this for at least 30 days. *The key is regularity*.

9) The impression you make on others plays a crucial part in winning and excellence. Be aware of how you dress, how you carry yourself, your tone of voice, what you say, and in general how you treat others.

10) Optimists have been shown to have more brain capacity than pessimists. Let your body work for you. Take

advantage of all the energy, lucidity and creativity hormones generated by consciously adopting and maintaining a positive attitude.

11) Stop using negative phrases. Your subconscious robot doesn't understand negative language; it records it as if you wanted it! Say what you *want,* not 'what you *don't want.* Say what you *can* do, not what you *can't do.*

12) The ABCs of self-determination are important factors for your success. The "A" is for accountability; *take responsibility for your actions!* The "B" is for blame; *stop the blame game and instead figure out how to improve the situation!* The "C" is for choice; while you may or may not be able to change external circumstances, *you can always change your internal response to any situation!*

13) Personal attributes play a powerful role in the achievement or non-achievement of success, and courage is one of them. The biggest obstacle to courage is fear, and fear is a product of your imagination. You can defeat fear in two ways. First, *positive visual simulation imprints on your subconscious robot in such a way as to literally create a feedback path for increased courage.* Second, take action toward accomplishing what you fear; *action actually reduces the fear associated with it.*

14) Learn to be adaptable. Uncertainty and change are normal and to be expected. *Peak performers not only anticipate change, but also reach out to embrace it before it overpowers them.*

15) Become customer-focused. The key things to remember here are: a) The purpose of business is to serve the customer; the by-product is profit; and b) *You can get anything in life that you want if you help enough other people get what they want.*

16) To accomplish the maximum, make use of synergism. *Cooperate, don't obstruct.* Remember that the cooperative whole is greater than the sum of our individual selves.

17) What kind of people do you associate with? Are you energized, encouraged and inspired by your associations? It's time for you to deliberately associate with winners! As a start, use this: *I have much to contribute, and the people I seek are even now seeking me!*

18) Take the High Road. Your success will be directly related to the degree you follow your own sense of what is right and avoid doing what you know is wrong.

19) Have Faith in yourself! Once you have firmly decided upon a goal, act in pursuit of that goal regardless of the supporting evidence. If you still have doubts, don't worry, it's okay. What's important is *for you to proceed as if you have no doubts.*

20) A trait of highly successful achievers is the ability to keep commitments, made to others or to themselves. A commitment to trying this system for 30 days is not life-shaking. Nevertheless, it is a promise to yourself and a reflection of your integrity. No excuses and no rationalizations. *If you are really serious about achieving success, this is how you must treat all commitments you make from this day forward.*

This is a summary of many of the important points presented in this book. But these aren't a substitute for the reader Action Steps given at the end of each chapter. It is essential that those steps be performed on a regular basis as a part of this program.

The items listed here constitute a considerable amount of information in highly condensed form. As you read and then review these points, a picture of the entire scope of this program will emerge, and I believe you will see how they all fit together. If you follow this program, your success and the achievement of your highest and noblest dreams will be...inevitable.

EPILOGUE

Many people say to me, "I wish I could be like you. If I had your confidence, I would do it." In view of this, I would like to remind you where I came from.

I started out in life at a very low point. When I was in the first grade I vividly remember my teachers asking me to leave the classroom and sit in the hallway with the other slow students. I was in the first grade for two years; I couldn't keep up with the rest of the class. This was followed by years of remedial reading classes. I tried very hard but was always playing catch-up.

Later on, I was frequently the victim of bullies. I was skinny, and where muscles should have been, my arms and legs looked like broomsticks. When I became nervous, which was often, my throat became clogged and I had to take special medication just to be able to talk.

What kind of self-esteem and confidence does a kid like that have? None! I hated being bullied and I hated being afraid.

I gradually became more determined to conquer fear. In high school I had a true friend, Lorenzo, who was very strong and able. One day I was being bullied by some juniors and seniors, and they knocked my books down the steps as I was going to class. Later, when I saw Lorenzo, I said, "Will you teach me to fight?" "Yes," he said.

He came to my home and we went into the basement. He had brought boxing gloves with him. We put them on and he said, "Put your hands in front of you and defend yourself." Lorenzo sparred with me but I knew he was holding back. "Lorenzo," I said, "try to hit me. I want you to."

He said, "No, Richard, I don't want to hurt you."

I shouted back, "I don't want to be weak anymore! Hit me!"

He did. I woke up on the floor. Knocked out. I said, "What happened?"

He said, "I hit you."

I hadn't even felt it. I picked myself up and said, "Okay, I've got it now. Try to hit me again."

He knocked me out again. I was on the floor.

Finally, after many hours of practice and lots of bruises, I became more competent at defending myself.

When I took my college board exams I failed miserably. My mind had gone blank from fear. When I returned home after taking the exams and lay in my bed to rest, all the answers to the college board questions seemed to appear on the ceiling. My fear was gone and I could think.

My poor grades prevented me from going to the state college but I was able to start at Worcester Jr. College. While there I once again worked on conquering my fears. Two ways I did this was by becoming a body builder and mastering the art of self-defense using Karate as my vehicle. Strong muscles and lightning speed. No bully would ever frighten me again.

When I was at Worcester Junior College I took a speaking course. During my first talk I was terrified, and my brain went blank once more. I somehow managed to get through my talk, but I have no idea what I said. After that speaking course I told myself that one day I would be great. I would be fearless. I would be a wonderful speaker.

I had Faith, but there was no evidence to back it up.

After transferring to Worcester State College I did student teaching at a regional high school. It was a disaster. My voice was weak, my bearing was meek and spitballs were flying all over the class—there was no control. My supervisor advised me to quit. A month later he came back to review my progress. I had planned to show a movie and then have the class discuss it, but just as my supervisor arrived, one of the 10th grade boys grabbed the movie reel and rolled it down the hallway and the supervisor nearly tripped over it. "Out of control," his expression said. He told me that he would have given me an F in student teaching, but I hadn't quit and that was worth something; so I got a D. In spite of these and many other problems, I managed to graduate with a teaching degree.

I was pumped up and ready to be a teacher. In 1969 I went to my home town and saw the school superintendent, and he asked for my college records and two references. When he saw my "D" in student teaching, plus the fact that none of my references felt that I could do the job, there was not much for him to say except "No."

I pleaded with him to give me a chance. I told him how I'd always been a slow-starter in life and that my brothers were fine teachers and it was in my blood. He hesitated, but then admitted that one of his second grade teachers was sick, and maybe...just maybe...I could fill in for her.

Well, I did, and I was great! I went into that classroom full of Faith, and it worked. Some of the other teachers looked in on my class and told the superintendent I was doing just fine. That was the first of many substitute teaching classes, and they were followed by regular classes, and I was good enough to receive tenure in only three years!

Shortly after that I quit teaching to take a challenging sales job. Once again, I did poorly at first, but I had Faith in myself. From the worst salesman on staff, I became the best over three years. I moved up to Regional Director and then to Vice President. In 1977 I started my own company and began to present Peak Performance Motivational Rallies.

I'm telling you all of this to demonstrate something very important. I began as a meek, frightened boy, totally lacking in self-esteem and self-confidence. I was constantly bullied and my fear of inadequacy caused me to freeze in every situation where I needed to perform. Time after time I was told that I couldn't make it. But the more they told me I would fail, the more I was determined to succeed. Most people look at adversity as a reason to quit; I look at it as a test of my Faith in myself.

With the passage of years, I have now been a professional speaker and performance coach for 25 years. I took the greatest adversity in my life—lack of confidence and fear of speaking in front of people—and turned it into the greatest asset of my life.

Some people say to me, "If I could speak like you, I'd be doing the same thing you are." I say to them, "Where were you when I was growing up with the confidence of a salad bar? Where were you when I had to study long hours every night, repeating lessons over and over because the only way I could get them was by endless repetition?"

Faith in myself has made me fearless. My company now does white water rafting, and outward-bound-type adventures in which people climb 75 feet into the air and stand on a telephone pole. Heights used to terrify me, so I decided to conquer my fear. I also feared fire, so I attended a FireWalk seminar and walked on 1200° birch, oak and maple. I did the FireWalk over and over again because I feared it. I no longer will allow myself to be afraid. Today, *I* teach the FireWalk. I empower others with the confidence to walk safely and not burn, and to conquer their fear.

As I end this book, I want you to turn away from me for a moment and look at yourself. No doubt you have much more talent than I was born with. If you are reading this book, you are probably intelligent, educated, articulate, experienced, socially adept, with a host of other natural abilities that came so hard to me.

So you are starting out with several advantages. Yet these natural and learned talents, by themselves, are not guarantors of high achievement and success. Schools do not teach you how to do visual success simulation, how to mentally think, speak and act your way to great achievement; nor do they teach you how to gain courage, adaptability and Faith in yourself, to name just a few of the attributes of winners.

Think for a moment about the ideas presented in this book. Can you see that the procedures I have described are unlike any other self-development program? What causes an athlete to become a champion? What causes a teacher to become an inspiration? What causes a soldier to become a hero? What causes a businessman or businesswoman to become a dynamic CEO? What causes a politician to become a great statesman?

Listen: High achievers become high achievers not because of facts they have learned or physical skills they have honed or how smart they are. They become high achievers because of how they use their minds! *Whether or not you become a high achiever will depend on how you use your mind!*

The tools are right here and right now. Opportunity is knocking on your door. Can you hear it? Is anyone home?

God bless you and all your endeavors. I have Faith in you. Are you willing to have Faith in yourself?

Excellence In Leadership

By Richard Tosti
3 CD Video ROM Album
or 3 VHS Video Album $199.00

Excellence in Leadership
by Richard Tosti   3 Video CD-ROMs

Here is Richard Tosti's complete seminar video-taped. As a supplement to the book, it's awesome because you see and hear all the dynamic stage effects, and the audience participation is superb. It's truly the BIG SHOW! During this energetic, high content presentation, Richard Tosti shows you how to achieve and sustain a high performance level. You will learn a competency model of high achievement, with focus on: Visionary; Accountability, Empowerment, Excellence, Synergistic Team Player, Change Orientation, Adaptability, Customer Focus, Motivation/Initiative and Interpersonal Communication Skills. You will learn how to effect permanent behavior change. The end result will enhance your personal productivity, create a more positive and productive work environment, and improve profits and team productivity. If you are a manager and you would like an inexpensive way for your staff to experience the full thrust of Richard Tosti's program, this is an ideal way to do it.
(Order form is last page in book.)

Excellence In Leadership

By Richard Tosti
3 CD Audio Album $69.00
or 3 Audio Cassette Album $59.00

Here is Richard Tosti's complete seminar in audio form, recorded live before 100+ management/sales people. As with the video albums, this is a supplement to the book. You will learn how to achieve and sustain a high performance level. You will learn a competency model of high achievement, with focus on: Visionary; Accountability, Empowerment, Excellence, Synergistic Team Player, Change Orientation, Adaptability, Customer Focus, Motivation/Initiative and Interpersonal Communication Skills. You will learn how to effect permanent behavior change. The end result will enhance your personal productivity, create a more positive and productive work environment, and improve profits and team productivity.

This album is an excellent inspiration while driving. You will experience the excitement and the enthusiastic audience responses, as well as the dynamic sound effects. It is a heart-pounding, spine-tingling presentation that you will listen to not just once, but over and over again!
(Order form is last page in book.)

Fly High With Wings of Courage

By Richard Tosti
4 Audio CD Album $69.00
For Teenagers

This seminar provides a dynamic, inspirational way of teaching young adults the essential character traits, habits and behaviors that will guarantee success. The program includes building self-esteem, confidence, self-respect and self-control. Among the many other topics are teaching positive self-direction and positive self-discipline, adaptability, perseverance, courage, communication skills, patience and the power of faith. With this album, Richard Tosti supplies the necessary skills that are lacking in much of the modern world, and does it in a way that captures the attention of and inspires teenage listeners.

(Order form is last page in book.)

By Richard Tosti
12 Audio Cassette Album $129.00
For Ages 5 to 10

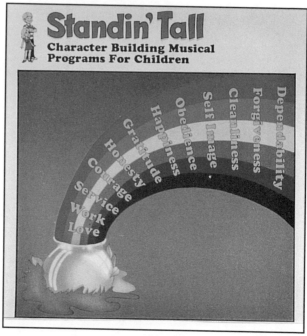

The twelve vital topics in this uplifting series become part of the children as they participate in the highly entertaining, dramatic story narratives and the beautifully performed, fully orchestrated songs. Side A of each cassette contains the complete program. Side B repeats the same program but leaves out the lines of the main child in the story, giving the listener the chance to read along in the twelve accompanying 24-page story booklets, say aloud the missing lines and actually become one of the cast. Topics include: 1) Obedience, 2) Honesty, 3) Forgiveness, 4) Work, 5) Courage, 6) Happiness, 7) Gratitude, 8) Love, 9) Service, 10) Cleanliness, 11) Self-Esteem and 12) Dependability
(Order form is last page in book.)

Creating Your Own World

By Richard Tosti
4 Audio CD Album $69.00
For Ages 3 to 10

Creating You Own World is a unique educational and instructional program to help children build their self-esteem and reach their full potential. The CD album features music, sound effects and a cast of five unique characters led by Spokes, the friendly comic hero who learns to overcome personal challenges and difficulties common to young children. Also included is a 90-page Picture Book sequentially designed to help reinforce the spoken concepts. As the storyteller engages Spokes and the other characters through the dramatic episodes, each child will learn how to best handle life's challenges.

(Order form is last page in book.)

Order Form for Additional Copies of
The Proactive Path
by Richard Tosti

1-99 copies . . . . $16.95 each

100-999 copies . . . . $14.95 each

1000-4999 copies . . . . $12.95 each

5000+ copies . . . . $10.95 each

Total No. of copies ordered _____

Total product cost $ _____

For MA shipping addresses, please add 5% for tax $_____

Shipping cost: Please add $5.50 for 1st copy and $1 for
each additional book sent to same address . . . . $_____

Total amount due $_____   Amount enclosed $_____

Method of payment ___Check ___ Visa ___ MasterCard ___Amex

Card No. _____ Expiration Date _____

Please make checks payable to Tosti Associates.

**Tosti Associates, 45 Pickman Drive, Bedford, MA 01730
781 280-0750 (voice), 781 280-0732 (fax), CPI3030@aol.com (email)**

Your name (please print)_____

Shipping address_____

_____

Order Form for Richard Tosti Albums

Excellence In Leadership

		Each	Total
3 Video CD ROM Album . . . . . . # Copies_____		$199.00	$_____
1 VHS Video Album . . . . # Copies_____		$199.00	$_____
3 Audio CD Album . . . . # Copies_____		$ 69.00	$_____
3 Audio Cassette Album . . . . . . # Copies_____		$ 59.00	$_____

Fly High With Wings of Courage

4 Audio CD Album . . . . # Copies_____		$ 69.00	$_____

Standin' Tall

12 Audio Cassette Album . . . . . # Copies_____		$129.00	$_____

Creating Your Own World

4 Audio CD Album . . . . # Copies_____		$ 69.00	$_____

For MA shipping addresses, please add 5% for sales tax $_____

Shipping cost: Please add $5.50 for 1st copy of each item
and $1 for each additional item sent to same address $_____

Total amount due $_____   **Amount enclosed** $_____

Method of payment ___Check ___ Visa ___ MasterCard ___Amex

Card No. _____ Expiration Date _____

Please make checks payable to Tosti Associates.

Tosti Associates, 45 Pickman Drive, Bedford, MA 01730
781 280-0750 (Voice), 781 280-0732 (Fax), CPI3030@aol.com (email)

Your name (please print)_____

Shipping address_____

_____

Notes

Notes

Notes